DIARY

An Intimate Description of the Natural History of
Glacier Lake and the Cirque of the Unclimbables,
in the Words of Scientists Who Were among the
Area's First Pioneers

with a Foreword by
David Raup

edited by
John Harris
Vivien Lougheed

Repository Press
2002

Acknowledgements

Excerpt from George Goodwin, reprinted with permission of Natural History (Dec. 1937), copyright the American Museum of Natural History. Excerpts from the Canadian Alpine Journal reprinted with permission of the Canadian Alpine Journal and the Alpine Club of Canada. Excerpts from Hugh Miller Raup's article "Botanical Exploration of the Mackenzie Mountians," in the Arnold Arboretum Bulletin of Popular Information, and from Hugh Miller Raup's The Botany of Southwestern Mackenzie reprinted with permission of the Arnold Arboretum, Harvard University. Recipes from Lucy Raup's The Camper's Cookbook reprinted with permission of Charles E. Tuttle Co., Inc. of Boston Massachusetts and Tokyo, Japan. Journal entries of James Soper and Hugh Raup reprinted with permission of James Soper and David Raup. Material by Dick Shamp, Donald Flook, and George Scotter reprinted with their permission. Excerpts from interviews with R.M. Patterson, Bill Clark, and Gus Kraus printed with permission of the Senior Heritage Programs Officer, Parks Canada. Permissions pending for Hugh Miller Raup's obituary from The Canadian Field Naturalist, for the excerpt from Harry Snyder's Canadian Geographical Journal article, and for Norm Thomas's story "Man against the North."

Thanks to the College of New Caledonia for production assistance.

Cover photo: Vivien Lougheed.

ISBN O-920104-24-X

Order directly from:

Books & Company
1685 - Third Ave.
Prince George, BC
V2L3G5
Phone: (250) 563-6637
Fax: (250) 563-6610
Email: BookSales@books-and-company.com

INTERVIEWS

OBITUARIES

BIBLIOGRAPHY

FOREWORD: A Small Boy on Glacier Lake

By David Raup

I was barely six when we flew from Ft. Simpson to Glacier (né Brintnell) Lake in June of 1939. Some recollections are still sharp though much is lost or, more likely, distorted by time. So I will stick to the sharpest memories, like the flight in. I remember lying on top of the load, up near the ceiling. Most seats and anything else moveable had been taken out to make room for our food and gear. Approaching the lake, the plane seemed to dive steeply - though it was probably only banking sharply to circle down. Still, it was pretty scary.

My brother Karl (age 9) and I were not allowed to bring toys because, it was said, toys would add too much weight and volume. But we made do. Jack knives made almost anything possible. My favorite pastime that summer was lying in a willow thicket by the lake shore using my knife for elaborate logging operations. The only rule was that the knife could not be used if I had more than two Band-Aids on my fingers.

And there was always water to play in! In 1939 and many subsequent summers in the Arctic, water provided hours of entertainment. Streams could be dammed or diverted and pretend boats could be floated downstream and perhaps attacked by missiles from the shore. If the pretend boats were punky sticks, they would often send out little lifeboats after a direct hit. In the lake, anything that would float, and have rocks thrown at it, was fun. Another rule: I could play by the lake only if both pairs of pants were dry.

Karl and I didn't have to work much around camp. Our parents thought kids should play while they could. There were some chores, of course. Hauling water in canvas buckets to be hung on a spruce limb by the fire. And cutting and hauling some

wood. The worst, though, was the daily job of mixing pow-
dered milk. Klim was, and probably still is, an awful substitute
for milk.

I don't remember the mosquitoes being bad, although I suppose
they were. After late summers, I remember packing away all
the summer clothes because the smell of smoke was too strong
for life in Boston. Before DEET, smoke was the only defense.

Every three or four days that summer, the whole party left camp
for collecting. Usually going up! Karl and I sometimes helped
in the collecting, especially finding lichens for Mother, but this
was neither required nor encouraged. Mother and Pops, as pro-
fessional botanists, had the idea that their kids should not be
coerced into following in their footsteps. Karl had a collection
of minerals and I caught butterflies when I could - but this was
done almost in secret. Strange. The collecting trips were usu-
ally fun but sometimes pretty wet and cold. Lots of climbing.
Mother often sort of pulled me, with me gripping a stick she
held behind her. Not much real help but it felt good. Pops
always carried the rifle on these treks. He had been chased by
a bear some previous summer and was always a bit nervous,
especially as we used game trails whenever possible. Coming
down at the end of the day was always fun, especially racing
and sliding down the vast scree slopes.

The only time I know of that Pops ever shot the rifle was when
he got the moose. Almost every evening (or so it seemed),
Mother and Jim Soper went fishing from the canoe. They
almost never caught anything but one evening they sighted a
moose on the far lakeshore. Karl and I were in our tent - sup-
posedly asleep - when Pops came for the gun. We were not
allowed out. A bit later, we heard a half-dozen shots in quick
succession. It was always claimed that Pops fired only a single
shot but we knew better. The alleged echoes were a family joke
for years thereafter. Ever fearful of grizzlies, Pops hung the
butchered carcass from a tree, still on the far side of the lake.

A week or so later, Pops and Jim towed the remains by canoe to the far end of the lake to get it even farther from camp.

The rifle was not our only armament: we also had a rather primitive bow and a couple of arrows. I remember it being used only

Glacier Lake from the top of Frost Creek, 1939. Photo: Hugh M. Raup

once to shoot the radio antenna up into a tree, or perhaps to the high cache. The antenna was fine but the radio almost never worked. The radio's purpose was to send weather reports to Simpson and to call for the plane to pick us up, especially in case of medical emergency. Our principal medical support was a can of stewed tomatoes "in case someone gets sick," Mother said. All other food, except bacon and ham, was dried and stored in waxed cloth bags. I don't remember the tomatoes ever being eaten.

The moose was a welcome relief. The ham and bacon we had been living on was moldy and salty. It had to be scraped and parboiled before it was even barely edible. The bacon tins did enable us, however, to fix the canoe left by the Snyder party in 1937. Karl and I spent hours collecting spruce gum to glue and caulk the tin and canvas that we used to fix the great hole in the center section of the canoe. We never knew why the canoe had been left on the ground rather than up on the high cache away from sitting bears.

The trip out in August was marred only by problems of taking off. The plane was too fully loaded to take off downwind - the only feasible direction given the terrain at the upwind end of the lake. Many tries. We would load up, go to the head of the lake, rush downwind, and then back to shore to unload some more stuff. Success finally came after starting the takeoff upwind, getting on the "step," and then pivoting down to complete the job downwind. I think everybody was pretty nervous.

Then came the long trip back to Boston. Wonderful days on the sternwheeler on the river, the MacDonald Hotel in Edmonton, and the always fun trip to Ottawa on the train. The dining car was the best part. Back to school, with building anticipation of getting out a bit early in the spring to head North again. My only complaint in those years was that if I had been home in the summer I could have joined the boy scouts.

INTRODUCTION

by John Harris

Glacier Lake, in the geographical heart of the NWT's Mackenzie Mountains, is a mecca for rock climbers and for canoeists on the upper South Nahanni River. The climbers fly into the lake. The canoeists, usually on outfitted tours, hike up to the lake from the river, unlock canoes that outfitters have chained to trees, and paddle up the lake. At any time in mid-summer, up to forty people are likely to be camped at a hospitable delta on the north shore at the west end of the lake.

The big attraction is not the lake, beautiful as it is. All of today's visitors to Glacier Lake are coming for the Cirque of the Unclimbables, north of the lake. The Cirque is, really, four, small, parallel cirques that include a dozen vertical granite walls of about 800 - 1000 meters each, topping out at about 2500 meters of elevation. The entrance to the Cirque is guarded by the 1000-meter wall of Mt. Harrison Smith, or the Cathedral -- after which the range of granite intrusions that includes the cirque was once named. The Cathedral towers over the west end of Glacier Lake and is visible from the Nahanni. To the north of the Cirque is Mt. Sir James MacBrien, at 2674 meters the NWT's highest peak.

However, this majestic cluster of rock faces wasn't discovered by climbers until the Fifties, and the flow of climbers and canoeists didn't begin in earnest until the Sixties. Before that, Glacier Lake attracted quite a different type of visitor: the scientist. Starting in 1934, Glacier Lake became the window through which Canadian and American scientists examined the geology, flora and fauna of the western NWT. After the war, these studies were built upon as geologists, wildlife specialists, and even the U.S. Defense Department used the lake as a base in completing comprehensive plant, mineral and wildlife maps and inventories of the Mackenzie Mountains.

The first to arrive, perhaps the first non-aboriginal to set foot on the lake's shore, was mammalogist George Gilbert Goodwin, Assistant Curator at the American Museum of Natural History in New York. The AMNH is probably the premier natural history museum in the U.S. -- not as large as the Smithsonian but better. Goodwin authored a number of books, for the Museum, on the wildlife of Central America and the Caribbean, and provided a great number of entries (on mammals: Tasmanian Devil, Tapir, Water Buffalo, Bison, etc.) for Collier's Encyclopedia, 1950-1980.

Goodwin was accompanied, and financed, by AMNH and National Museum (now Canadian Museum of Nature) patron Col. Harry Michener Snyder, Fellow of the Royal Geographical Society, an Ohio-born financier headquartered in, at various times, Montreal, Sundre Alberta, Calgary and Tucson. Snyder arranged financing for North America's first radium refinery at Port Hope, Ontario; this refinery provided uranium for Canadian and American programs during the Second World War. Snyder's colonelcy was honorary, from Canada's Black Watch. Snyder was also an ardent big-game hunter; in 1950 he published Snyder's Book of Big Game Hunting, containing anecdotes of his hunts in various parts of the world (including the Mackenzie Mountains) and giving advice to those taking up the sport. Some of that advice involves getting permits to shoot trophies for museums; in his book, Snyder reprints the National Museum documents that accompanied his permits to acquire tropies along the Nahanni River and around Glacier Lake.

Snyder felt an attachment akin to ownership for Glacier Lake and its adjacent mountains and glaciers. He was, according to Pierre Berton in The Mysterious North, the first white man to see the Cirque and the rugged peaks around it, "a range of sawtooth mountains encompassing one of the largest snowfields in Canada. They rose like a great triangular island above the ocean of mountains surrounding them."

Snyder and Goodwin's 1934 visit was brief, a mere reconnaissance. They were busy elsewhere at the time, on what the AMNH called the First Snyder Canadian Expedition. They were collecting specimens in Wood Buffalo National Park at the west end of Lake Athabaska. But they took enough time from this to fly in and reconnoitre. They identified a good campsite -- the same one used today by the canoeists and climbers.

They also began to attach names to prominent features. There's no record of the exact progress of naming, and some of the names stuck for only a few years, but they named the lake Brintnell Lake, after Leigh Brintnell, the pilot who flew them in and founder of Mackenzie Air Services, a company backed by Snyder. Snyder took to calling the mountains around the lake, now known as The Ragged Range, the Snyder Range. The mountain, the north-east shoulder of which forms the lake's south shore, was The Colonel Mountain. A higher peak to the west was named Mount Ida, after Snyder's wife. The mountain directly behind the campsite became Red Mountain, and the creek running off it down through the campsite into Glacier Lake was Frost Creek. Frost Creek also drained Terrace Mountain, to the east of Red Mountain.

Mount Ida is still Mount Ida. The Colonel, Red and Terrace Mountains and Frost Creek are not on the topographic maps, but the names are in common use among outfitters and climbers. Brintnell's name was taken off the lake but remains attached to the large glacier above the lake, to the main feeder creek from the glacier out into the Nahanni River, and to a smaller lake between Glacier Lake and the river.

In the following year, 1935, Snyder and Goodwin were busy on their second Snyder Canadian expedition, collecting more wood-buffalo specimens, as well as specimens of musk-oxen in the Barrens to the east of Great Slave Lake and of black-tailed (or dark-phase) white sheep along the lower Nahanni. There was no reconnaissance at Glacier Lake that year. In 1936

Snyder flew in to take aerial photos of "the Snyder Range," but weather prohibited. He waited for three days and then left. His partner Goodwin was in Central Asia that year, on the Morden Graves North Asiatic Expedition, securing specimens of Siberian tiger and saiga antelope.

In 1937, on the AMNH's Third Snyder Canadian Expedition, Snyder and Goodwin came by riverboat up the Nahanni to Virginia Falls, and then by float plane from the Falls to Glacier Lake. With them were Howard Frederick Lambart of the Canadian Geodetic (now Geological) Survey, with his assistant Karl Stein of New York.

Lambart was a registered land surveyor who had started his career in 1917. He was also a serious mountain climber, vice-president of the Alpine Club from 1924 to 1926. Prior to his visit to Glacier Lake, he spent seven years in charge of the Yukon-Alaska boundary demarcation, climbing Mt. St. Elias to 16,500 feet before being driven down by weather. He topped Mt. Natazhat (13,480') and later was a member of the five-man team that first summitted Logan. His published work includes studies of the glaciers of the Pacific Coast ranges and accounts of topographical explorations of Mount Logan and the Rockies from Yellowhead Pass to Jarvis Pass.

The group started triangulation studies, cutting a base line along the lake and building signal stations on seven adjacent high points, one of them The Colonel, or Colonel Mountain, which Lambart and Stein climbed on July 26 - 27. They took infrared photos to establish contours. They measured the lake's elevation (2600'), length (5 miles), width (1/2 mile) and depth (175'). All of these figures are reported by Goodwin. Two years later, a Harvard expedition estimated the lake's length at 3 1/4 miles, and was told by Snyder that the lake's depth was over 1000 feet.

Goodwin took samples of fish (lake trout up to 16 lbs, and grayling), and of local fauna including caribou and bears. He also ran a trapline at the upper end of the lake to acquire as many kinds of small mammals as possible. The National

Museum hit list included groundhog, marmot, squirrel, chipmunk, mouse, shrew, bat, porcupine, pika, pack rat and vole. Snyder himself, who hung around for only ten days of the six weeks spent by the expedition at Glacier Lake, finally got his aerial photos, including some magnificent shots of the Cirque and the Brintnell Glacier. He estimated the icefield, of which the glacier is a part, to be slightly larger than the Columbia Icefield, about 60 miles long and 30 wide. He counted 11 arms, valley or hanging glaciers, radiating off.

The general results of the Snyder expedition to Glacier Lake, including a good selection of photos, appeared in popular magazines in 1937. Goodwin released his article in a publication of the American Museum, Natural History magazine, where his account of the 1934 and 1935 expeditions had previously appeared. At the beginning of his article, he explains his interest in Glacier Lake in terms that might escape the lay person and mystify the expert: "here we expect to find the missing link in the mutation of Arctic, Hudsonian, and Transition species." But apart from this rather technical beginning, his account is, like his previous one, chatty and focussed on actual events, with little said of any scientific significance.

Goodwin seems to have been interested mainly in the Nahanni River and Virginia Falls, and the colorful history of the entire area. He says, "I heard many weird tales, that bordered on the supernatural . . . . One outside story had it that a tribe of hostile Indians resent the intrusion of the white man . . . ." In Fort Resolution, Goodwin talked with trappers who warned him away from the Upper Nahanni/Glacier Lake area specifically. He quotes these trappers as follows: "'Why just over a year ago two fellows, well known here in Resolution, went into that country to trap. When they didn't return, a search was made by plane. Their cabin and outside camps had been burned, and the men were never found.'"

Snyder, in The Canadian Geographical Journal (presently Canadian Geographic), speaks more of scientific discoveries.

Though Snyder could not be taken as an authority, one assumes that the discoveries he mentions were confirmed by Goodwin. Snyder records the shooting, on the lower Nahanni, of many black-tailed Bighorn. He probably means Dall or Stone Sheep as Bighorn do not occur north of the Peace River. Snyder also records shooting, just north of Glacier Lake, a Barren Lands Grizzly and a Mountain Goat, both of which species were hitherto, he says, not thought to inhabit the Mackenzie Mountains. This may have been considered correct at the time, though the grizzly, originally referred to as the Barren-Grounds grizzly, is no longer thought to be a distinct species. The extensive photos published with Snyder's article show that the lake and its environs, including the Cirque, look much the same now as they did then. The Brintnell Glacier has shrunk back considerably from its outlet down Brintnell Creek, and most of the tributary ice pack has melted out of the Cirque.

Lambart, in The Canadian Alpine Journal, writes the clearest and most detailed article. As his "Short Historic Sketch" shows, he was even more deeply immersed than Goodwin in the colorful events of Nahanni history. The "Sketch" tells the story of the legendary McLeod Mine, sought along various tributaries of the Nahanni River, especially the Flat River, by famous mountain men like Albert Faille, R. M. Patterson, Gus Kraus, Bill Eppler, Bill Clark, and Dick Turner. His "Narrative" explains the riverboat trip to Virginia Falls, and the subsequent flight into the lake from above the falls. The riverboat trip was to collect specimens of sheep along the Nahanni. It was also a dream of Snyder's to navigate the entire river: "Snyder was anxious that entrance into the country should be made by the use of power boats ascending the South Nahanni River.... This would have been quite an impossible task." But the trip to the falls did enable Lambart and Stein to measure their height (300 vertical feet) and estimate the volume of water passing over (1200 foot-seconds). Lambart also provides the exact geographical locations and altitudes of all major features from Virginia Falls to Mounts Harrison-Smith and Sidney Dobson (just south of Glacier Lake). He announces that he is working on a contour

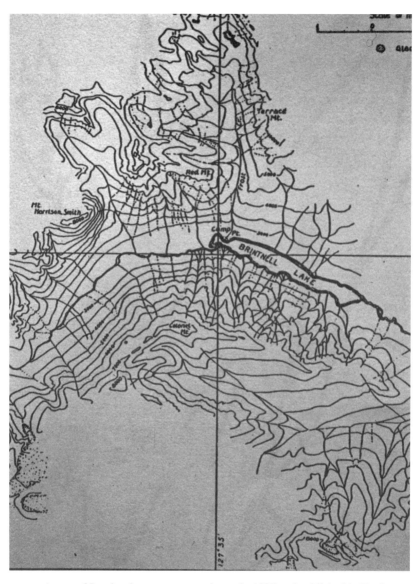

A part of Lambart's contour map, drawn in 1937 and published in Hugh Miller Raup's <u>Botany of Southwestern Mackenzie</u> (1947). Snyder sent the map to Raup in 1939. North of the lake, Mt. Harrison Smith, Red Mountain, Terrace Mountain, and Frost Creek are identified. Colonel Mountain is identified to the south of the lake.

map of Glacier Lake and its environs, including the Cirque, some hundred square miles of terrain. His map would be the first such map of any area in the Mackenzie Mountains.

The flora went unexamined, but that was remedied two years later. In 1939, Harvard's Arnold Arboretum mounted its own expedition, funded by Harvard, other U.S. Academies, and the National Museum of Canada. The primary objective of this expedition was clearly stated in the resulting publications: "to collect representative flora from what was then one of the largest blank spots in the plant maps of the northern part of the continent."

The expedition was led by Hugh Miller Raup, a Harvard professor who was to become one of North America's foremost plant geographers. Raup had already done studies around Lake Athabaska (1926, 1932), Slave River and Great Slave Lake (1927), Wood Buffalo Park (1928, 1929 and 1930), and the Peace River from Finlay Forks to Lake Athabaska. Later, he would study plants along the Alaska Highway, from Dawson Creek to Whitehorse in 1943 and Whitehorse to Fairbanks in 1944, and still later he would work in other parts of the Canadian north including Baffin.

On his 1939 trip to Glacier Lake, Raup took his family with him -- his wife, Lucy, lichenologist, and their two sons, Karl and David. The younger son, David, only six years old at the time, became one of America's foremost paleontologists. He retains vivid memories of this trip. Hugh Raup's field assistant was James H. Soper, recently graduated from McMaster University after completing his Masters degree in Botany. Soper went on to do his Ph.D. at Harvard, with Raup as one of his supervisors, and then to become one of Canada's great field botanists, a professor at the University of Toronto and later Chief Botanist at the Canadian Museum of Nature.

The research of Soper and the Raups was, after World War II, written up by Hugh Raup and published, by the Arnold Arboretum, in 1947. Entitled The Botany of Southwestern Mackenzie, this accessible 275-page book is a primary source of information on plants of the southwestern NWT. The Harvard team located and mapped mosses, lichens, and vascular plants, and catalogued vascular plants, some 725 species and varieties. To provide a cross-section of vegetation through the entire Mackenzie Mountains, Raup uses A.E. Porsild's studies of plants along the newly-built Canol Road, as well as older studies of plants along the Mackenzie and around Great Slave Lake -- studies that date back to John Richardson's during the first and second Franklin Expeditions.

But the book is much more than a catalogue of plants with maps of plant locations and accounts of likely origins and spread. It is a comprehensive description of the Mackenzie Mountains and, more particularly, the area around Glacier Lake. It begins with the history of exploration and mapping, and then proceeds to explain the conditions that make for the various plant communities that Raup describes. Raup details the origins of the rock strata of the mountains, including the massive granite intrusion that he refers to as the Snyder Range. He describes glaciation in the area, the effects on the terrain of the last ice age and of the valley glaciers that survive into the present. A part of Lambart's manuscript contour map, provided by Snyder, is used in this section. Next, weather patterns are described -- temperature, cloud cover and precipitation at the lake compared to Fort Simpson. The history of fires in the area is specified. In about 1887, Raup says, one fire swept up and to the east of Frost Creek. There is evidence of a much earlier fire on the north shore closer to the centre of the lake.

Raup pays special attention to the plant communities in the alpines above the lake (each slope different), in the hanging valley (once a tributary glacier) above Frost Creek, in the entire "valley" of Frost Creek from lake level to the alpines, in the flood plains (caused by beaver dams) at the top end of the lake, and in the half-dozen or so alluvial fans that occur around the lake and provide comfortable camping spots and close facsimilies to beaches. He describes a "remarkable" feature of the lake, the "rich forest of spruce" that covers the surrounding slopes for a distance of 500 meters above the Lake: "The spruce attain breast-height diameters of 2 - 3 feet, heights of 60 - 100 feet.

James H. Soper on Glacier Lake in 1939, sketching Mt. Harrison-Smith.
The raft was provided by the Snyder Expedition of 1937.

Their grain is twisted and at their bases they have a large amount of compression wood on their down-hill sides. They are bent to vertical at the base because of land-slips and snow slides."

Visitors to the lake, especially those who make their way from the lake to the Cirque, will note and applaud the accuracy of Raup's conclusion about this spectacular forest: "The shrub layer is not dense, and offers but little hindrence to travel through the woods. The principal difficulties of travel are the rough, bouldery substratum and the tangle of fallen logs that are everywhere in the way."

In his catalogue, Raup's most elaborate descriptions are of vascular plants that he has never before seen outside of the Glacier Lake area. Some of these plants get localized names: *Poa Brintnellii* (Brintnell's bluegrass), *Picea glauca Porsildii* (Porsild's white spruce), *Carex Soperi* (Soper's sedge) and (Snyder would've been happy) *Arnica Snyderi* (Snyder's arnica). According to the Canadian Field Naturalist, all of these are bona fida additions to the plant catalogue.

Lucy Raup's lichen collection waited some time for study. It was donated to the Farlow Herbarium of Cryptogamic Botany at Harvard, in 1978. The collection was in good condition despite having been stored in the Raups' garage for decades. The specimens, about 600 of them, were unprocessed, meaning they were (a) not pressed, (b) not labeled, (c) not divided into duplicates, and (d) mostly unidentified. Scott LaGreca, curator of lichens, noted that some of the identified specimens were not identified correctly, and some species were collected over and over. As he understands it, Lucy had no formal training in lichenology, but had considerable experience. Her experience was mostly with the lichens of northeastern North America, so that the Glacier Lake lichens may have been a bit beyond her. However, he recognized the importance of the collection, and so did others. The collection was borrowed by Teuvo Ahti, at the University of Helsinki in Finland. Ahti kept it from 1978 -

1990, for a project he was working on with George Scotter, a Canadian Wildlife Service biologist working in the Nahanni area. Scotter had sent some lichens to Ahti to be identified, using Lucy Raup's collection as a reference. All in all, Ahti and his colleague Orvo Vitikainen identified about 60 specimens in Raup's collection. They wanted to do all of the collection, but ran out of time. The collection sat for another decade, and then LaGreca began to identify and process the specimens, and sent duplicates to other herbaria. He is at present working on a paper about Lucy's collection. Some specimens are still waiting at Farlow for identification by interested workers.

Both Raup and Soper kept journals of their stay at Glacier Lake. Soper has photocopied his diary, with some photos, and makes it available to anyone who asks for it. Raup's diary is lodged, with his Canadian papers and photos, at the University of Alberta's Book and Record Depository. Both men report how the team came in with Mackenzie Air, which took them to the same spot selected by Goodwin and Snyder. They set up for two months of botanizing, June 16 - Aug 20. They repaired a sectional canoe left by Snyder's 1937 expedition. The canoe had been smashed up by a grizzly (one of David Raup's most vivid memories is of him and his brother collecting and melting the spruce gum used in the repairs). They circumnavigated the lake. At the lake's outlet, along the north shore, they saw, in Soper's words, "the remains of a cabin and a good cache still standing." Raup specifies that the cabin was "burnt." This was their only evidence of possible occupation on the lake that might precede Snyder and Goodwin. They met Snyder, who flew in one day to check on the camp. Snyder, who always had a cook with him, invited the Harvard team to share in the delights of his camp kitchen. Snyder and his friends hunted and fished, unsuccessfully, and flew out the next day. Raup shot a moose, a welcome addition to the camp larder, and Lucy and Soper canned the meat. As Soper describes it, all camp chores were shared -- though the canning and cooking was carefully supervised, and the special (and eagerly anticipated) desserts provided by Lucy Raup. She later published The Camper's Cookbook (Tuttle

1967), a popular early guide to camp cooking distributed in Canada by Hurtig.

Glacier Lake was quiet then, through the war and after, for over a decade. In mid-June of 1952, Dick Shamp and Norm Thomas flew in from Watson Lake with famed flying trapper George Dalziel, a Nahanni mountain man who'd taken to the air. Legislated out of the trapping business in 1937, he took to commercial flying and established a base at Watson Lake. The large log house in Watson Lake, across from the log hotel, was Dalziel's, and he built a similar one, also still in existence, at the south end of Dease Lake, where his daughter Sherri Bradford still operates his guiding/outfitting operation.

Shamp was a civil servant in Washington DC, an air photo interpreter with the air-photo arm of the U.S. Geological Survey. The Survey needed to find a way to distinguish snow from reindeer moss (cladina lichen) on the photos provided by the Royal Canadian Air Force. Shamp had contracts with the Catholic University of America to correlate vegetation patterns with air photos, and provide information on how to move troops through a subarctic environment like (and this is Shamp's example) Kamchatka. Also, the Pentagon wanted him to test the U.S. Force's survival equipment in a subarctic environment. Mainly, Shamp intended to prospect, having seen interesting faulted structures and zones on the aerial photos. These were near Shelf Lake just north of the Cirque and above what is now called Bologna Creek. Thomas was a friend of his, a professional photographer from Phoenix Arizona.

With them was a Yale University biology student and member of the Yale Mountaineering Club, Howell Martyn. Martyn was the vanguard of a group of Yale mountaineers who called themselves the Yale Logan Expedition (YLE), after the range of the Mackenzies that includes the Cirque; Martyn and his roommate at Yale, Dudley Bolyard, were arranging an expedition to hike in the Logan Mountains, and climbing Harrison-Smith was the main objective. Martyn had accepted a job with Shamp and

Thomas in order to save money for the YLE; Dalziel would be able to bring in the rest of the YLE, with all the supplies and equipment, three weeks later, and take Shamp and Thomas out. Without this arrangement, it would've taken two flights to get the YLE in with the supplies and equipment. In addition, Shamp paid Martyn $100.

The contact between the YLE and Shamp was Hugh Bostock of the Geological Survey. In preparation for their trip, Martyn and Bolyard, a student of geology, had visited Bostock in Ottawa. Bostock was a recognized authority on the geology of the Yukon and adjoining parts of the NWT. He was also in contact with Shamp.

Shamp acknowledged that his expedition was a failure as a prospecting trip, though he also said that it was the experience of a lifetime. He told the Edmonton Journal that he "found some mineral deposits, but not in quantity worth worrying about." The Catholic University got its report, which discusses two things: (1) how small units of soldiers - i.e. reconnaissance units - should choose routes through subarctic areas using aerial photos, and (2) how to deduce the actualities on the ground from what appears in the aerial photos. Part 1 of the report is a good summary of what an experienced hiker would know about moving through mountainous areas in the north, and would prove useful to anyone unfamiliar with the terrain. Part 2 is made up of side-by-side aerial and ground photos, with commentaries on each set of photos. The survival equipment got a thorough test, through three weeks of near steady rain. The rations -- dehydrated meat bars, pea soup, hot chocolate -- were a resounding success. Without them, Shamp, Thomas and Martyn might not have made it. But Shamp's report on this topic is not available.

Shamp's team made a three-week, circular trek north, following Frost Creek up and over a high pass which afforded grand views of the backside of the Cirque and Mt. Sir James McBrien. They descended what they called "Martyn Creek" to its outflow

Howell Martyn on his way up Frost Creek, 1952, with the Shamp/Pentagon Expedition. The giant gold pan was soon lost, followed by the Geiger counter and the rifles.

on what they called "Thomas Creek" which drains Mount Mulholland and the Brintnell Glacier and flows into the South Nahanni. Instead of descending "Thomas Creek" to the Nahanni, when they realized how much of a trek they had undertaken, they stuck to their plan and went up the creek, over another high pass and down what they called "Dog Leg Creek," now known as Bologna Creek. Bologna drains out of the north end of the Brintnell Glacier and enters into the Nahanni River across from the Island Lakes. They suffered various mishaps on the creek, losing their rifles, gold pan, rope, and Geiger counter. Shamp fractured his shoulder blade and cracked his knee-cap in a roll down Bologna Creek. At the Nahanni River, they built a raft using rope, shreds of canvas, and even shoe laces. The raft broke up a couple of times, and they lost more equipment, including two sleeping bags, their watches, and a tent, but eventually made it close to the mouth of Brintnell Creek. From there, they hiked back up their camp at the east end of Glacier Lake. A couple of days later, Dalziel arrived with the rest of the YLE, and Shamp and Thomas flew out.

The details of this journey were set down in an unpublished story, "Man Against the North," by Norm Thomas. Thomas intended to sell his story to a popular magazine and added some fictional touches, mainly a confrontation, on the high pass over Bologna Creek, with a grizzly. Apart from this his account is, according to Howell Martyn, accurate. Thomas also took a great number of beautiful photos, using a fifteen pound box camera that shot 5x7 negatives. These photos amount to an impressive achievement, a photo-documentary of the Glacier Lake/Bologna Creek area as it appeared fifty years ago. Shamp published some twenty of these photos in his report, and indicated that he had more in his files.

Most of the YLE team - which included John Cristian Bailar III, George Yntema, and Harry Nance as well as Martyn and Bolyard -- were there to climb, but Bolyard had additional plans. Bolyard was especially interested in glaciers. During the Ottawa visit, Bostock pointed to two areas in the Mackenzie

Mountains, saying that practically nothing was known about the geology of these areas. He encouraged Bolyard to go to the Mackenzies and report back to him about what he learned.

Bostock's comment about the Mackenzies was later illustrated by one of Bolyard's professors, Carl O. Dunbar, who was a paleontologist and, together with his mentor, Schuchert, was famous for constructing paleogeographic maps for the various geologic time units of North America. Bolyard asked Dunbar to identify a particular graptolite (*Didymograptus* sp.) that Bolyard had collected on the north flank of Sidney Dobson. Dobson informed Bolyard that he'd made an important discovery, which was that the Ordoician Sea had occupied that part of the continent.

In the mountains around Glacier Lake, Bolyard collected samples, data, and photos for the dissertation for his bachelor's degree. Much of this material was collected in a short expedition from Glacier Lake along the west side of Sidney Dobson, down into the Rabbitkettle River Valley and up and down that valley for some distance. Entitled "Preliminary Geologic Reconnaissance of the East Central Portion of the Logan Mountains, NWT," it contains 26 pages of text, with 16 color photos, a geologic map, and four annotated oblique aerial photos, one of Harrison-Smith. The dissertation cites work by Bostock, Dave Kingston (on stratigraphic reconnaissance along the upper South Nahanni), and Raup. Unfortunately, both Yale University and the Canadian Museum have lost their copies of Bolyard's work.

While the YLE was climbing south of Glacier Lake, Snyder returned, for the last time it seems, on August 4, 1952, and stayed until August 29. He had with him his new wife Louise, two hunting friends and a guide. Once again he had obtained special permits: this time the plan was to collect caribou specimens for the National Museum. The Federal Government, when it approved the permits, assigned a young biologist of the Canadian Wildlife Service (CWS), Donald Flook, to accompany Snyder. Flook was 24 years old, just one year out of university, and stationed in Fort Simpson -- the first and last CWS biologist headquartered there. He was there from 1951 to 1954, and his terms of reference made no mention of the Nahanni, most of his attention being devoted to the Mackenzie Lowlands where almost all native hunting and trapping took place. But CWS interest in the Nahanni was growing, and Flook's work at Glacier Lake turned out to be the first of a number of CWS studies at the lake, two completed by Flook and two by his successor in the area, R.C. Stewart. Further CWS incursions into the Mackenzie Mountains were made in connection with the establishing of Nahanni National Park. George Scotter and Norm M. Simmons were the officers who undertook most of this research.

Flook's report, entitled "H. Snyder Expedition - Upper South Nahanni River, August 1952," is eight pages long. It uses Raup's book to provide a general description of the lake, outlines the make-up and activities of the Snyder Expedition, includes a daily diary, and finally details Flook's "Wildlife Observations." Appended are nine somewhat fuzzy black and white photos, most of Brintnell Creek, which Flook calls "Rapids River," from the lake up to the glacier. The photos were taken when Flook joined John Bailar and John Yntema on a hike delivering supplies to the YLE. There's also a photo of Snyder at his customary campsite at the lake's west end, and of the two caribou specimens taken, one by Snyder's hunting friend H. N. Jennings, a medical doctor from Calgary, and one by Glen Kilgour, the team's guide, outfitter, and cook. Snyder, who was suffering medical problems and could not easily get around, had to content himself with shooting a black bear that invaded his tent. This too Flook photographed -- it has a light-colored mane -- along with samples of the fish he took in a gill net at the mouth of Frost Creek.

In 1953, Flook returned on a winter trip. He was surveying for marten with Mackenzie Mountain Game Preserve Chief Warden Bill Day. Their guide was Gus Kraus, a prospector, trapper and guide established in the Nahanni watershed since 1933. The hotsprings on the Lower Nahanni, just below First Canyon, are named after him. The three men landed on Seaplane Lake and McMillan Lake near the upper Flat River, and then on Glacier Lake. Flook reported to CWS that Yukon trappers were obviously poaching marten on the upper Flat River; he and Kraus noted signs of occupation in the disintegrating cabins built there years earlier by Faille and Kraus himself, and found no trace of marten. At Glacier Lake, however, Flook found a healthy and undisturbed marten population. In a five-mile circle from camp down the lakeshore and up the slope to about 500', Flook estimated that there was a substantial population of martin in residence.

Flook pointed out that the 1937 federal government ban on airplane trapping [aimed specifically at Dalziel-eds], had backfired, rendering the upper Nahanni and Flat areas inaccessible to Native trappers of the NWT. The upper Nahanni had been abandoned, and the upper Flat was being poached out by trappers from the Yukon.

R. C. Stewart's two reports have been lost.

George Scotter made three trips into Glacier Lake, in 1970, 1971, and 1974. These were part of his ongoing studies of the Nahanni/Flat River valleys. Scotter has published extensively on this area, some 15 magazine articles and scientific papers and 6 unpublished reports for CWS. His published papers are available through the Edmonton Public Library. Scotter was intrigued by the area and spoke extensively with (and took photos of) its inhabitants - for example Gus and Mary Kraus at Kraus Hotsprings. Scotter's photos of Glacier Lake and Hole-in-the-Wall Lake were used as calendar pictures in the 1970's. He corresponded with R.M. Patterson. He collected old maps of the area, one of which appears on the inside covers of David Finch's R.M. Patterson: A Life of Great Adventure (2000). On one of his trips he was accompanied by a CBC film crew led by Garnet Anthony, a CBC conservation reporter working out of

Edmonton. Anthony recorded about five hours of interview with Gus Kraus. The pictures taken at Glacier Lake, however, including some rare footage of mountain goats, were lost due to a camera that had been set out of kilter in the First Canyon of the Nahanni, when the cameraman fell into a cave.

As part of his work for CWS, Scotter co-chaired (with N.M. Simmons) studies commissioned by the federal government with a view to creating a new park in the Nahanni/Flat River valleys. Scotter and Simmons were told to plan a park of about 500 square miles, recommended 6,250 square miles, and got 3000 square miles. Two of the major losses were Hole-in-the-Wall Lake and Glacier Lake and their environs. Scotter and Simmons worked with two other officers, S. C. Zoltai and H. L. Simmons, to produce The Ecology of the South Nahanni and Flat River Areas (1971). This report went to Prime Minister P. E. Trudeau, who took a special interest in the park project and, before the park was set up, canoed the South Nahanni River.

The report recommended that park headquarters be at Nahanni Butte (they are presently at Fort Simpson), and that there be campgrounds at the mouth of First Canyon, in Deadmen Valley, at the mouth of the Flat, at Seaplane Lake (up the Flat), at the Water Survey cabin above Virginia Falls, and at Rabbitkettle Lake (close to the fabled hotsprings, and acting as trailhead for routes into both Hole-in-the-Wall and Glacier Lakes). Concerning Glacier Lake and the Cirque, the report strongly suggested that the area be protected from destructive use. Three arguments are presented for including Glacier Lake and its environs: the significance of the Cirque for climbers, the fact that Glacier Lake is one of the few large lakes in the area, and Raup's historic work at the lake.

Scotter, in his scientific studies, made extensive use of works by Raup and Soper. Scotter in addition knew Raup personally, having traveled through the arctic with him for three weeks in 1959. Since The Botany of Southwestern Mackenzie did not catalogue mosses, Scotter limited his collections to those. Part

Nahanni dress code, summer 1952. Ollie Rollog
dropped into the YLE camp for a visit.

of this work is presented in "Bryophytes of Nahanni National
Park," <u>Canadian Journal of Botany</u> 55 1977): 1741-1767. In the
Annotated List of Species at the end of this article, Glacier Lake
is identified as site 54. In this area, among the liverworts,
Scotter collected *Ptilidiaceae ciliare, Blepharostoma tri-
chophyllum, Lophozia ventricosa and Cephalozia bicuspidata.*
Among the mosses he collected *Sphagnum girgensohnii,*

Tortella fragilis, Cratoneuron filicinum, Drepanocladus revolvens, Hypnum lindbergii and some dozen others.

Scotter and his colleagues also catalogued the area's birds. This work appeared as <u>Birds of Nahanni National Park</u>, published by the Saskatchewan Natural History Society. Scotter provided the sightings at Glacier Lake and supplemented these with sightings mentioned by Flook.

Some questions, about this era of scientific activity at Glacier Lake, remain unanswered, and are perhaps unanswerable. First: Will it eventually be possible to retrieve the missing research done by Bolyard and Stewart? Shamp too may have produced more reports, and Karl Stein, Lambart's assistant, may also have written about the area. There's also a possibility that Snyder took pertinent materials and photos with him when, as an old man, he left Canada for Tucson. It is known some of Snyder's records and trophies were lost, in 1955, when his ranch house in Sundre burned down, but R. M. Patterson, who maintained a correspondence with Snyder's widow, believed that some material survived and would've gone to a museum in Tucson.

Second: Were Goodwin and Snyder the first people to visit the lake? They assumed they were. Lambart says there was no evidence of Aboriginal occupation and Raup, who had some training in identifying archaeological sites, says the same. It should be remembered, though, that neither party was actually looking for such evidence, and no archaeologists were present.

As to white occupation, Goodwin says in his 1937 article that, "a little over a year ago," two trappers went in, burned their cabin, and never made it out. This is the burnt cabin mentioned by Raup and Soper in their diaries, located, according to them, on the north side of Brintnell Creek, just below where the creek leaves the lake. RCMP reports say that this cabin was last occupied by two trappers, Bill Eppler (sometimes spelled Epler) and Joe Mulholland, who flew in from Nahanni Butte with Dalziel in February of 1936, and failed to appear as scheduled at Nahanni Butte in May. Their plan was to carry their pelts down

Howell Martin on the mysterious cache at the low end of Glacier Lake.
Remains of the burned cabin were seen by Soper and Raup in 1939, but
had disappeared by 1952.

Brintnell Creek to the Nahanni, build a skinboat, and paddle down to Nahanni Butte where the Nahanni flows into the Liard. Since no rifles, traps or human remains were found in the wreckage of the cabin, and since the bottom two rounds of logs survived the fire, police deduced that the cabin burned in winter when the snow was high against the walls, and the men died trying to walk out the Nahanni.

By 1952, when the YLE arrived, the cache was still there and repairable, but none of the students noticed the burnt remains of any cabin. These must have disintegrated in the 13 years since Raup noticed them. The YLE did encounter a couple of prospectors, named Slim and Ollie. According to Donald Flook, these were Ollie Rollog and Slim Raider (exact spellings uncertain). They'd flown in earlier with Dalziel and walked and paddled an improvised canoe to Virginia Falls. There, they (and a third man, David Aoncia) had been picked up by the Associated Airways flight coming for Flook and Kilgour (the rest of Snyder's party had departed on an earlier flight) and brought back to Glacier Lake. Flook mentioned that Rollog and Raider were old timers with some experience in the area, but there was no talk of any lost trappers or burnt cabin. Martyn is certain that Dalziel made no mention of any cabin.

Dalziel, in an unpublished manuscript left in possession of his family, says that he knew about this cabin before he took Eppler and Mulholland to it. He did not build it; he disapproved of the use of cabins in trapping, regarding them as dangerous. Dalziel didn't get his plane until 1935, but in 1933 and 1934 he became famous for criss-crossing large parts of the Nahanni watershed, trapping on the move and/or exploring. He could've been in the area before or shortly after Goodwin and Snyder, and discovered the cabin on Glacier Lake.

It's almost certain, then, that the cabin was built before Snyder and Goodwin turned up in 1934. Trappers, white or Indian, would have built it. One candidate is Albert Faille, who first entered the Nahanni country in 1927 and who put cabins in many places on the lower Nahanni and up the Flat. He was also known to travel regularly along the upper Nahanni in search of the lost mine. The police interviewed Faille about the disappearance of Mulholland and Eppler, and there's no record that Faille mentioned building the Glacier Lake cabin.

The third question concerns Snyder, whose support was pivotal to the investigations of Goodwin and Lambart, and of considerable value to those of Raup, Soper and Flook. What were his real motives? The Nahanni mountain men, who saw much of Snyder through the thirties and forties, found him to be an engaging personality, but basically thought he was using Goodwin and the others to get permits to shoot big game. Gus Kraus says, "the only way he could come in was by getting a permit for research. That was his excuse to get permits." Snyder's article mentions the permits, "graciously" given to him by the NWT Council. These must've been permits for hunting animals in a game preserve. The permits were issued by the Council on the advice of the Department of Mines and Resources in Ottawa, and that Department in turn sought the advice of the Chief Biologist at the National Museum. The Chief Biologist's response, published by Snyder in his book, was enthusiastically in favor of issuing the permits. Snyder had already, it was noted, donated a Wood Buffalo group and three Bighorn Sheep to the Museum, and the Museum "is badly in need of good specimens of adult mountain Grizzly, and of Mountain or Woodland Caribou, for mounting."

Kraus does suggest another motivation for Snyder: "He wanted his name on the Cathedral Range. If he spent $40,000 on exploration and turn it [the results] all over, they'd change it. I saw one map with that name on it, only one." If Kraus is correct, Snyder's plan backfired.

Flook defends Snyder, saying that he made a contribution to knowledge of the area. David Raup also defends him. Raup says of the AMNH: "Throughout the first half of this century it benefitted greatly from wealthy big game hunters who funded

expeditions like the one to Glacier Lake. It was a good arrange-
ment in that the patrons got a certain respectability for their tro-
phy hunting and the Museum got lots of dead animals for taxi-
dermy so that magnificent dioramas could be built as exhibits.
And some science came out of it also. Teddy Roosevelt was a
prime example of the enthusiastic patron -- and mighty hunter.
And he undoubtedly attracted others to the practice. The same
practice still goes on... except the patrons are outfits like
McDonalds and Disney and the trophies are videos, big
dinosaurs, and PR for theme parks."

The Canadian Museum and the AMNH certainly benefitted
from Snyder's largesse. In its catalogue, the Canadian Museum
has no memory of Snyder, but the AMNH website mentions
him as a patron and details his activities. After the Glacier Lake
expedition, for example, they list "the Snyder East African
Expedition" of 1938. One of the results of that expedition was
a 35mm film, shot by Goodwin, available now on cassette, that
shows among other things Masai costumes and customs, ele-
phants browsing, and Snyder posing with the gigantic tusks of
an elephant and being carried around on the shoulders of
natives in celebration of the hunt. Snyder had one of the tusks
mounted on an ebony base and included, in his hunting book, a
photo of himself with the tusk.

A fourth question: Did Lambart investigate the Cirque and do
any climbs? According to the historical records collected by
Nahanni National Park, he climbed Harrison-Smith or the
Cathedral, with George Roberts. Roberts was a Fort Simpson
trapper-prospector who, in 1937, was hired by Snyder as a boat-
man to relay supplies up the Nahanni to the falls. He proved
exceptionally competent and congenial, and was flown into
Glacier lake with the rest of the group. Bill Clark, Roberts'
close friend, reported that Roberts "climbed to the top of
Cathedral Mountain and put a cairn [there], with Lambart."
This would make Lambart and Roberts the first to climb in the
Cirque, and it is an attractive idea that one of Canada's pioneer
climbers could be so credited. But Lambart himself says noth-

ing of what peaks, besides The Colonel, were climbed in the process of setting up the signal stations. In his article, he presents a photo of Harrison-Smith and says of it "this peak we tentatively called Cathedral Peak which, with an altitude of 8340 feet above sea is 5740 above the lake." But it seems there was no signal station on Harrison-Smith, and one assumes that, had Lambart climbed the Cathedral, he would have said so.

Except for Scotter's work in connection with the establishment of Nahanni National Park, and assorted visitations by geology crews and scientists working for mineral exploration companies and the Geographical Survey during "Operation Nahanni" in 1963, the era of the scientists at Glacier Lake ended with the advent of the climbers, and the rapid spread of the Cirque's reputation as a climbing destination. The Yale students were the first serious climbers in the area. They climbed all the major

Dudley Bolyard prepares to explore the Brintnell Glacier to the west of Mt. Ida

peaks of Sidney Dobson, the huge massif that extends from Glacier Lake south to the Rabbitkettle River. They climbed Ida and explored the Brintnell Glacier to the west of Mt. Ida. They entered the Cirque, late in the season, and climbed what turned out to be the western peak of Cathedral or Harrison-Smith. They had hoped to find access to the main peak by that route, but found themselves separated from the peak by an ice-covered col. They had run out of time, by then, to attempt the front face of Cathedral; it was snowing heavily when they slid down out of the Cirque and back to the lake. Their exit preceded a major slide; while waiting at the lake for Dalziel to fly them out, the YLE witnessed the collapse of part of the face of Cathedral.

Bolyard's article, "The Yale Logan Expedition," published in 1953 in The Canadian Alpine Journal, alerted the climbing community to the possibilities, and the rush was on.

TRAIL GUIDE: Flat Lakes (Tungsten) to Glacier Lake

by **Vivien Lougheed**

This one-way route could easily be completed in twelve to four-teen days. For those really gung ho, it could be done in ten. Estimate your likely time carefully and give yourself an extra few days. It would not be good to miss your return flight from Glacier Lake.

Your flight out must be arranged in advance. Piggy-back onto another flight that is taking canoers to Rabbitkettle Lake or the Honeymoon Lakes. That way the pilot can drop off the canoers, pick you up, and take you back to the Flat Lakes before making his return trip to Fort Simpson, Blackstone, or Watson Lake. It makes the cost less. We flew with Jacques Harvey of South Nahanni Airways, and the flight back to the Flat Lakes via a round-trip tour of the Cirque of the Unclimbables was well worth the cost.

This hike should not be done with fewer than four people as there is no help along the way should an accident occur. We went in with six people and it turned out to be perfect. There were enough people to keep our humour up and the chores at a minimum for each person. This in turn kept us from getting too tired and having an accident. Also, weight is more efficient with two to a tent and with items like repair kits, first-aid kits, saw, stove, and pots serving everyone.

The route requires bushwhacking and route-finding abilities, advanced skills in river crossing, and the stamina to be in the bush for a long period of time. Once committed to this trip, there is no exit except possibly going all the way down the Rabbitkettle River to the lake, where there is a warden's cabin and a lot of river traffic, but that could be a tough hike.

Obligatory top-of-pass/objective-in-view photo. Vivien Lougheed and
John Harris on shoulder of Mt. Ida, July 1999. Brintnell Creek below,
and Mt. Proboscis in background.

From Mt. Ida, the Brintnell Glacier in the background, Brintnell Creek flowing through a rocky canyon down towards Glacier Lake. Cross Brintnell Creek on the gravel wash area visible where the creek braids. The log may still be available (for those with nerve) just up from the gravel wash. This wash was once close to a terminus of the glacier (see previous map), and was the site of the YLE base camp while they explored the ice.

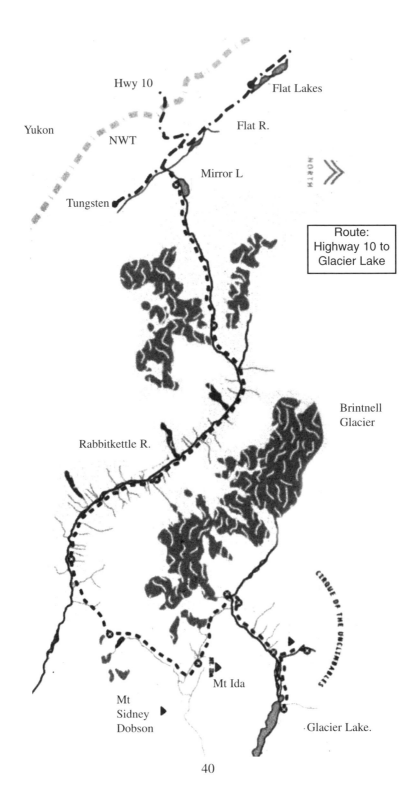

Hwy 10

Flat Lakes

Yukon

Flat R.

NWT

Mirror L

Tungsten

NORTH

Route:
Highway 10 to
Glacier Lake

Brintnell
Glacier

Rabbitkettle R.

CIRQUE OF THE UNCLIMBABLES

Mt Ida

Mt
Sidney
Dobson

Glacier Lake.

The bushwhacking is difficult above Mirror Lake and moderate on the Rabbitkettle River. Some ascents are very steep and one descent is difficult. You will always be a long way from a rescue, so take care never to travel when tired, as that is when most injuries occur. Take your time and enjoy the sensational scenery. We averaged 8 kilometers per day.

Topographical Maps: Shelf Lake 105-I/1 (1:50,000), Mount Sir James MacBrien 95-L/4, Mount Sidney Dobson 95-E/13, Dolf Mountain 95-L/3 (only for going to Rabbitkettle Lake).

Equipment Needed: You must carry enough food to last the two weeks of travel plus enough to hold you until your plane arrives. The flight could be delayed due to bad weather for up to a week, so plan for this possibility. Dehydrated soups are good for times when you are waiting, not working. Creek-crossing shoes are needed as the Flat River and Brintnell Creek are both long, difficult, cold crossings. The smaller unnamed creeks and the upper Rabbitkettle can be managed without shoes. Your tent must be leakproof and your sleeping bag must be warm. Expect snow on any one day and rain every day. On the other hand, you could have two weeks of blazing sun, in which case you will need lots of sunblock. The long days (about twenty hours of daylight) make sunny days extremely hot. The sun is directly overhead for many hours of the day. A location finder is nice but not necessary if your map-reading abilities are good. The landmarks are so extreme in this area that you should never be lost. Stove and fuel are necessary for at least three days of alpine travel where there is no wood. A nylon tarp makes rainy periods bearable. We spent a couple of rainy half-days under the tarp, and we waited two days for our plane to arrive. Part of that time was spent listening to the rain patter onto the tarp.

In this description I use map co-ordinates to give the exact location I am describing. Since this hike is not along a road, more exact locations are needed. The first number of the co-ordinates corresponds with the horizontal line on the map; the second number corresponds with the vertical line. Their intersect is at the bottom left-hand corner of the square on the map. The distances in this description are in kilometers and are approximate.

The Route:

0.0k Leave your bikes in the cabin or car across from the cabin located at the Flat Lakes/Tungsten Road junction (Shelf Lake 79-35). Shut the door and close the back window so animals won't get at your gear. Walk almost two kilometers towards Tungsten to a curve in the road (Shelf Lake 76-36). From there go into the bush towards the cutbank on the other side of the Flat River. During the bushwhack you will encounter a couple of small creeks that will have to be jumped. If you go towards the river north of the cut bank you will have to slog through swamp. Once at the Flat River, walk upstream past the rapids and the curve to a wide section. The rocks are slippery and the water is swift. This difficult crossing will take time.

4.0 k After crossing the Flat River, bushwhack your way up the hill. Veer slightly towards the lake but do not go down the slope onto the creek that drains the lake. Not far past that creek, and on the hill above the lake, is a cabin (Shelf Lake 77-37) partially eaten by porcupines. The cabin is a nice refuge if there is rain. There is a good stove and an axe. If you have started late in the day, the cabin is the best place to camp. When leaving the cabin, follow animal trails along the lake's south shore.

5.0 k There are boulder-strewn slopes at the east end of the lake. These must be negotiated carefully, making it slow going. Stay low as much as possible. It is advisable not to go too high on the slope, as you must come down to get past some cliffs. Stay on the south side of the lake and creek. The bushwhacking starts in earnest between the hill above the lake and continues to the gravel bars on Kuskula Creek (Shelf Lake 78-41).

8.0 k Before the gravel bars there is a waterfall and a small canyon that must be scrambled around. You must cross one skookum creek that comes down from the south. It is fed by the glacier above. Although there are some camping spots at the east end of the lake, the gravel bars on Kuskula Creek are recommended, as wood, flat spots, wildlife, water and scenic vistas are abundant. Also, sleeping is better when bushwhacking is over. From the cabin on the lake to the gravel bars on Kuskula takes about six hours. Once on the bars we put on sandals and walked up the creek rather than in the adjacent bush.

13.0 k At the upper end of Kuskula Creek are two glacier-fed lakes set in a moonscape (Shelf Lake 79-46). The glaciers are partly visible. The area is hospitable for a lunch break during sunny weather but bleak during rain. To reach the Rabbitkettle River, pass the two lakes and walk over the ridge directly to the north of the second lake. Once at the top, follow the creek, which you will see from the pass. There are camping possibilities along this creek. Stay on the north side of the creek; due to its water volume, you must cross the Rabbitkettle River above its confluence with this creek.

15.5 k A deep canyon on this creek, with sheer cliff walls and a raging torrent of glacial water passing through, is your next landmark (Shelf Lake 80-49). Once close to the trees, pick your route and bushwhack down to the river. The Rabbitkettle Valley looks inhospitable and difficult, but in fact it is fairly easy when compared to the bushwhacking above Mirror Lake.

17.0 k Cross the Rabbitkettle where the water is still clear and then cross the creek coming in from the north. If you are walking this route from the Cirque, follow the Rabbitkettle River until its water becomes clear as opposed to glaciated. Then go up and over to Mirror Lake.

Once across the Rabbitkettle River, go directly up the gravel bank close to the edge of the creek and look for an animal trail.

Stephan Biedermann on shoulder of Mt. Ida. Brintnell Creek below,
Cirque towers on the other side of the ridge opposite.

The one we found was so distinct I thought it must be an old horse trail used by prospectors (Shelf Lake 81-50). Follow this trail down the Rabbitkettle River, past numerous creeks, using the two large rock glaciers (Mt. Sir James MacBrien 80-53 and 76-56) that spew into the river as landmarks. The trail disappears near swamps, but it is well worth your time to drop your packs (with someone standing guard over them) and look for the trail again on the opposite side. The bushwhacking is horrid and slow without a trail. If unable to find it, go back to the river and cross into the bush in a diagonal direction until the trail crosses your line of walking.

29.0 k This is the Rabbitkettle canyon (Mt. Sidney Dobson 73-58), which must be climbed around, but you need not go very high to get past. Once over the canyon, the river opens up and gravel bars become abundant.

30.0 k Camping anywhere along these gravel bars is not only easy but delightful. Travelling downriver, continue in and out of the bush as necessary. Pass the curve on the Rabbitkettle and go down to the creek you will ascend to reach the plateau beside Mount Sidney Dobson (Mt. Sidney Dobson 69-67). The valley across the way is wide and protected at its entrance by a distinctive pyramid-shaped mountain.

43.0 k This creek is recognizable because of the two huge towers of sand-coloured stone with a passage in the center that looks intimidating. The climb is steep and a few scree spots are slippery. Carry water. It will take from two to three hours to get up onto the plateau. Once out of the bush, the walking becomes much easier. From here to the descent to Brintnell Creek, you are in one of the most beautiful alpines I have ever seen.

48.0 k There are camp spots on the plateau before the lake (Mt. Sidney Dobson 72-70), but if you can make it to the lake for camping, the scenery is spectacular. There is a hanging glacier at one end of the lake that occasionally drops ice cubes into the water. I have never been on such a stunning plateau. There is a grizzly who lives up here with her cubs, but she is wild and terrified of humans.

54.0 k Skirt the second large lake (Mt. Sir James MacBrien 76-71) along its north shore and then cross diagonally over the hill beside the lake to the next creek. Do not go too high, because on that creek there are cliff walls that are not easily descended. This creek leads to Mount Ida and lies in a wide, open valley.

57.0 k There is pleasant camping from the junction of the three creeks (Mt. Sir James MacBrien 78-71) all the way to the top of the main creek, which lies in the shadow of Mount Ida. Once on the large flat plateau beyond the headwaters of the creek, you will get your first view of the Cirque. It is from this plateau that Galen Rowell got his world-famous photo of Proboscis, one of the towers in the Cirque. You will also see Brintnell Glacier and Creek, including the wide gravel bars where the creek levels off. This is where you will cross Brintnell, unless you are a high-wire expert and want to try the famous log bridge (see 62.0 k).

58.0 k Getting down off the plateau and onto Brintnell Creek is a challenge. The map is incorrect. The tiny rock glacier that is shown on the map (Sir James MacBrien 78-68) is not there. To get off this mountain, go to the vegetated arm at the northwest corner of the plateau. Going down the creek bed on the west end of the plateau is intimidating and unsafe. The descent will take a few hours and in places packs may have to be lowered on a rope rather than carried. I lost the bum of my pants crawling down parts of this slope.

59.0 k Once on the little valley below the hanging glacier, the walking becomes easier. Continue down the valley along the moraine beside the creek until you are in the bush. Then veer to the west until you hit a second moraine. This one is made of rusty brown boulders. Cross over that and descend to the braided washout of a tributary to Brintnell Creek. Once across the washout, go to the flats beside Brintnell. Camping is excellent anywhere along Brintnell.

62.0 k Your trip is now just about over. Your last challenge is to cross Brintnell. If you go upstream you will come to a canyon with a log over the water. Some people are known to shimmy across, but the rushing torrent below is intimidating. We crossed downstream at the flats early in the morning, when the creek was at its lowest. You will need to navigate up and down the creek along gravel bars to get across, but it is possible.

67.5 k The creek that runs down the huge granite face of Mount Harrison Smith (Mt. Sir James MacBrien 70-84) comes from the entrance to the Cirque of the Unclimbables and Fairy Meadows. Go up the talus slope along the edge of the gray perpendicular wall. It is a steep ascent among huge boulders that are often tippy, and it takes a few hours to reach the top. There are some cairns showing the best way to go. Coming down along this route is not recommended.

69.5 k Fairy Meadows is exactly as its name suggests. It is a lush green meadow surrounded by huge pillars of rock and dotted with boulders the size of suburban houses. Walk through the meadow along a well-worn path towards the back of the Cirque, where there are two rock overhangs. Climbers have made these two places comfortable by placing rocks for chairs, hanging ropes for pack lines, and clearing flat spots for tents. The creek is close, but there are no toilet facilities, in spite of the area's large number of visitors. Be certain to hang your packs on the lines as the marmots and low-bush grizzlies will invade your gear, chew through your new $400 backpack, and eat your last chocolate bar.

Make this base camp and explore the Cirque with daypacks. You may never be in a more spectacular place in your life.

75.0 k To reach Glacier Lake campsite (and your flight out), leave Fairy Meadows by following the trail back to the upper creek crossing on the talus slope. From there, go into the bush and beat your way through the alder and willow to the spruce trees. It is a short (30 minute) bushwhack, but once in the forest there is no underbrush, the slope is gentle, and the vegetation underfoot makes walking easy. This route is much safer and quicker than descending by the boulders on the talus slope. Coming up this way would be difficult because fighting against the growth direction of alder is a nightmare. Going down this way means you never cross the creek flowing from Fairy Meadows.

Once down the steeper part of the mountain you will cross a trail or arrive back at the creek where there is a log to cross and a rope to hold on to. This is actually for those coming from Glacier Lake and going up to the Cirque. Follow the trail turning to your left towards Glacier Lake. At Glacier Lake there is a small cabin in which tents can be pitched. There is a large gravel bar in front of the cabin, with a clear water creek on each side of it. If you do not want to stay here, you may also cross the easterly creek and continue down the lake for a couple of hundred meters to a camping site tucked into the trees. The ground is flat and there are many camping spots. There is also an established fire pit with rustic furniture around it. The planes like to unload here on the small beach.

DOCUMENTS

From "The Snyder Mountains -- An Expedition by Power Boat and Airplane to Map an Unchartered Mountain Range in Northwest Canada and Study the Fauna of this Unknown Region," by George G. Goodwin, Assistant Curator of Mammals, American Museum. 1937. <u>Natural History</u> (Dec. 1937): 750-780.

The Snyder Range, which runs parallel to the Mackenzie Mountains in that great unexplored region north of the 60th parallel in the extreme western Northwest Territory, has been named in honor of Mr. Harry Snyder's extensive research work in this territory. The region visited on this summer's expedition is of special interest from a biological standpoint, as it is somewhere here that we expect to find the missing link in the mutation of Arctic, Hudsonian and Transition species. Owing to the inaccessible nature of the country, practically no scientific research work has been carried on between the Mackenzie and Yukon drainage.

In 1934, Mr. Harry Snyder and I made our first reconnaissance trip by air into this territory and formulated our plans for a study of the region. In 1935, we attempted to scale the white waters of the Nahanni by boat. Our craft was wrecked on its first trial trip in the rapids, but we did get to the Gates, using two 28-foot power scows, and gained our objective at that time -- specimens of the white sheep with black tails.

The Snyder Mountain Expedition of 1937 was made possible through the generosity of Mr. Harry Snyder, whose keen interest and unfailing persistence led the expedition through to success.

The Nahanni is a most beautiful but extremely turbulent mountain river, and I heard many weird tales that bordered on the supernatural, of trappers and prospectors who had ventured into this territory and disappeared leaving no trace; others were found dead. One outside story has it that a tribe of hostile Indians resent the intrusion of the white man, but we saw no trace of Indians, though we frequently came across the trail of some lone trapper who spends the winter in this barren wilderness. . . . [Albert Faille, most likely—eds.]

While waiting [in Fort Resolution] for fair weather, we visited a cabin where four or five trappers were living. They had 40 or 50 sled dogs tied along the lake front, and trapped mainly on the barren lands. Strong, hardy fellows they were; yet when we told them where we were going, they looked at us with a mixture of awe and pity. Did we not know that there was something wrong with that Nahanni? That in the last eleven years, thirteen white men had gone there never to return? "Why, just a little over a year ago, two fellows, well known here in Resolution, went into that country to trap. When they didn't return, a search was made by plane. Their cabin and outside camps had been burned and the men were never found. And take the McLeod boys: everybody knew what happened to them a few years ago up on the Nahanni. Their bodies were found; they had been shot and mutilated. All these men were thoroughly used to this country and were hard customers. There is a tribe of Indians up there that have decided not to let anyone into their country. Big, strapping Indians they are, too."

Crossing Great Slave Lake, we threaded through the eastern islands and cruised down the Mackenzie River to Fort Simpson. Here we . . . hired a boatman, George Roberts, and his pointer scow to transport the excess baggage.

While rearranging our supplies on the shore of the Mackenzie, a bank rising fifty feet above the river caved in and buried our outfit several feet deep under soft, sticky mud. On our way the next morning, we made good time to Twelve-Mile Island on the Liard, but there the motor on our hired boat failed, and had to be sent back to Fort Simpson. It proved beyond repair, and we preceeded with one of our spare 8-horsepower motors.

The 30 miles of rapids on the Liard were swifter than we had anticipated. We approached them early in the evening and Jim Ross, a tall, typical westerner in charge of the outfit, argued that if he spent the night thinking of those rapids he might not want to tackle them. So we pushed on. Hugging the cliffs and lining the boats where possible over the roughest water, we got over the worst rapids by six the next moning, when Sandy took over the helm and Jim took a much needed rest. That evening we sighted the Nahanni bluff and made the forks by dark.

The Nahanni River, averaging 200 yards in width, flows southeastward through wild country into the Liard. It has an average fall of eight feet to the mile. In places the current rushes fifteen or more miles an hour. The landscape is a jumble of rough mountains, irregular steep ridges, hills, valleys, and ravines.

A supply of 150 gallons of gasoline, which we had expected to find at Fort Simpson, was supposed to be awaiting us at the forks in care of a trading post. There was only one person here, a woman [eds-Daisy Mulholland most likely], who was in charge. Her husband had been in Edmonton for several months. Although our wireless showed that arrangements had been made with her husband to supply us with gas, she politely but firmly refused to give us any, stating that the wire was not from her husband. After considerable argument, however, and paying $2 per gallon in cash, she agreed to let us have it and we were able to proceed. We made relatively good time, as the days were long. Twice we were almost capsized when we struck submerged rocks in midstream. These rocks always seemed to be placed in the middle of the roughest water on the swiftest rapids.

The second day we arrived at the so-called Tropical Valley or Hot Springs, an area of not more than two miles radius of flat, mucky soil more or less covered with a thick undergrowth, with small grassy meadows. Hot Springs bubbled up about a quarter of a mile from the river bank, with a temperature of about 95 degrees F. The animal life in this strange environment, however, proved no different than elsewhere. One weasel taken was pure white, but it was an albinistic individual. Mice, voles, shrews, squirrels, and other small mammals were normal.

With engines racing full speed, we crawled out of the first canyon and camped on a sandy level above the river. Strangely enough we found two paddles here, one a new custom-built paddle, the other a home-made affair. There were also signs of a recent camp here. Indians would hardly leave their paddles, yet as far as we could learn, no one had been in this vicinity for some time.

Entering Dead Man's Valley, we jogged along with relative ease, and stopped at noon near the beginning of the second canyon, not far from where the McLeod boys were buried. The valley looked very calm and peaceful, probably much as it appeared to the McLeod boys until they were murdered. The fourth day we camped at the Gates, one of Nature's wonders. The walls of the canyon rise straight up for 800 feet and the river rushes through. The following morning we passed the Rapids of the Drowned, so named because a party of Indians lost their lives at this point.

All went well until we reached Hell's Gate, where the shaft on the 32-horsepower motor snapped. Strange as it may seem, this occurred in relatively deep water and was not caused by striking rock. From here we had to make relay trips with the small pointer scow to the falls. At Hell's Gate, the river makes a sharp right angle turn between sheer cliffs and the rapids dash headlong into the face of a rocky wall. Everyone who knew the river advised us not to try to run a loaded boat through Hell's Gate, but our boatman thought he could make it. Entering the rapids from the side, a surging, boiling current lifted the stern of the boat clear out of the water. With motors roaring and having no control, the boat was dashed against the cliff. The board holding the engines was ripped off and they went overboard. Fortunately, the current carried us into a backwater above the crest of the torrent, and the motors, attached by safety ropes, were pulled ashore.

We patched up the boat with spruce pitch and were soon humming onward, none the worse except for a good scare. The scow, however, leaked badly and the extra pressure of the swifter water made it extremely unsafe. In fact, the boatman expressed his opinion that the last relay he made was about all the boat would stand. Some of the party preferred to walk the remainder of the way over the rocky mountain ridges rather than attempt the hazardous trip by water. The last three miles of the rapids were probably the roughest and most turbulent section of the river.

Rounding a sharp turn, we came into full view of Virginia Falls. The splendor and beauty of this ponderous volume of water, as it roars over a a precipice and thunders 300 feet to the river below, are indescribable, and we gazed spellbound at the glory of it all. The falls, together with the rapids above them, make a descent of 390 feet. Right at the brink a huge column of rock divides the falls into two sections. The water drops into a many-colored, rock-walled canyon, and rushes on down and around a bend. Perched high on a rocky crag facing the falls, is the eyrie of a golden eagle. The falls, like most illusive things of the North, are moody, and retiring; shrouded for the most part in a veil of white mist, they break out into the bright sun-shine in all their splendor and beauty. The fog is swept aside, but only to creep back and draw the veil once more, throwing a perfect rainbow across the canyon.

The portage of one mile around the falls was very steep and dif-ficult. The first section was 100 feet up a small stream trickling over loose rocks, then through a marsh over a dry hilltop 470 feet above the river and down to the bank.

The next noon Mr. Stanley McMillan, of the Mackenzie Air Service, arrived in the Fairchild plane to fly us to Glacier Lake in our main collecting area in the Snyder Mountains. . . . An hour and a half in the air brought us to our destination, and we made base camp at the upper end of Glacier Lake. The plane returned to Fort Simpson to bring in a supply of gas for a recon-naissance of the region by air.

Glacier Lake, situated in the heart of the Snyder Range, is one of the most beautiful places in the North country. Its mirror surface and perfect silence, broken only by the cry of a loon, were a great contrast to the thundering falls. A white granite peak overshadows the upper end of the lake, its perpendicular walls towering 4000 feet. Next to this is a red mountain apparently saturated with iron. Springs spouting from its sides have stained the slopes with rust. Timber climbs 2000 feet above sea level. The lake is five miles long and about a half a mile wide, and has a measured depth of 175 feet. It contains plenty of fish, both lake trout and grayling. Some of the large trout landed tipped the scales at 16 pounds, and made a welcome addition to our larder.

The Snyder range is a regular mountain paradise. From Glacier Lake high mountain ridges extend as far as the eye can see in seemingly endless succession. Peak beyond peak, towering chimneys and vast ice-fields come into view as we scaled the mountain slopes. The numerous peaks more or less joined by narrow, razor-edged ridges average about 6000 feet, and the highest are probably not more than 10,000 feet.

Mr. H. F. Lambart, of the Canadian Geodetic Survey, and his assistant, Mr. Karl Stein, of New York, settled down to the difficult task of charting the mountains and putting them on the map. It proved considerably more of an undertaking to scale some of the peaks than appeared from the lake, for distances were most deceptive.

Loose rocks at the base of the granite pinnacle on the upper end of the lake, which seemed from camp to be about three feet in diameter, proved to be as big as churches. A base line was cut one mile long on the shore of the lake, carefully measured and posted. Observation stations were established on the surrounding mountain peaks. Almost continuously overcast sky delayed triangulation, and clear days, when we got them, necessitated 24-hour duty on instrument work. One of the flag-pole markers established a mile down the lake was continually being pushed down and we never did find the reason for this. Some ten miles above the head of the lake a glacier creeps down the mountainside, and beyond we discovered a vast hitherto unrecorded ice-field. Avalanches of rock and landslides were quite frequent around the lake. One afternoon in particular there was a continuous rumble in the mountains that lasted for a considerable length of time. Scanning the ridges across the lake, I saw a river of rock pouring steadily down a gulch, ploughing its way through the timber and down across a meadow to the creek above the lake. It was literally a river of rock, keeping within certain bounds, pouring from a seemingly inexhaustible source.

The first clear morning we started on our reconnoiter trip by air . . . . We flew over the ice-fields and got some good pictures. The grandeur and beauty of these mountains cannot be exaggerated. Clouds were rapidly closing in and by the time we landed, all the peaks were shrouded in fleecy white clouds. Running a trap-line at the upper end of the lake, I found fresh tracks of bear that headed straight for camp . . . . On inspection of the meat cache we found it had been torn apart and all the meat was gone. The following evening, as we anticipated, the bear again visited our cache.

A careful survey of the mountain slopes around the lake revealed two big billy goats on the high crags some 5000 feet above the lake. Looking them over with a 24-inch monoscope, they appeared to be very big fellows, but as they were barely through shedding their hair it seemed advisable to leave them for awhile. . . .

We scaled the ridge back of camp and over the saddle into what was apparently a good game valley. We made camp at the border of timber and pushed on the next day with a view to collecting about six miles further up, at the base of an iron mountain . . . . At the foot of the mountain there was a small lake, the outlet carrying a fair head of water which disappeared down a sink hole. Deep down in the crystal clear water I could see the skeltons of two bull moose with locked antlers. . . .

From "Exploring Upper Nahanni River and Snyder Mountains in 1937," by Harry Snyder. <u>Canadian Geographical Journal</u> 5 (1937): 169-190.

It is now 1937. Plans started last year have materialized. The Northwest Territories Council has graciously given me permits, and on June 1 a new party, as usual under the command of Jim Ross, with Mr. Fred Lambart, as chief geographer and scientist; George Goodwin, naturalist; my particular chum Colonel A. J. "Sandy" McNab of the U.S. Army (retired); and the crew, composed of Carl Stein, Lambart's assistant; Ted Boynton, the cook; and Jim Callao, are leaving Edmonton. . . . Then on to Fort Smith, where our new boat is waiting, continuing by river all the way up the Nahanni to Brintnell Lake and the Snyder mountains with 900 pounds of scientific instruments, a ton of grub, a half-ton of other camp equipment, and 500 pounds of cameras and film.

After a rather slow trip [the boys] reach Fort Simpson and engage George Roberts with his boat to help them up the Nahanni. They leave on July 1, and I have planned to meet them in the Snyder mountains on July 20.

July 20: Piloted by Stan McMillan, we leave in Mackenzie Air Service's new "Fairchild." We have a light load and Stan requests permission to take along the wife of a trapper who lives at Fort Simpson with her two babies. We are glad to do this. We have a pleasant flight to McMurray, and Ida (Mrs. Snyder) enjoys the trip, especially because she has the pleasure of taking care of the little child.

We stop at Fort Smith for the night because of bad weather . . . . Much to my surprise, last night, when we arrived at the hotel at Fort Smith, I found Poole Field waiting for some freight to take back to his little trading post near the mouth of the Nahanni. Shortly afterwards , George Dalziel, the flying trapper, arrived in his "ship." After a short talk, he decided to fly on to McMurray. Then in came Jack Stanier, the prospector who, like Ulysses, pursued his quest for twenty years, and in the end, with Leigh Brintnell's assistance, found the lost diggings of the McLeod brothers.

Each subsequent year, on my return to the North, I get the same old thrill from discussing northern lore and gossip with these already almost legendary heroes who have done so much to create the present North. Soon they will be gone . . . .

July 21: It is bright and clear this morning, and weather reports from the north are good, so we take off at nine o'clock and fly to Outpost Island, Ida and I still taking care of the little baby . . . . From Outpost Island, where I pick up our sectional canoe for the Nahanni river, we refuel the ship, and go on to Fort Simpson . . . . At 4 o'clock we take off from Fort Simpson, climb steadily and hit the Nahanni just below the first canyon. Our altitude is 7,000 feet . . . . We reach Virginia Falls -- a beautiful spectacle! Now we are over the Upper Nahanni. The cloud blanket is far to the west; and dead ahead, outlined against the northwest sky, are the jagged peaks of the Snyder range. Pictures are taken from either window of the plane; and there, directly over the lake, again we see that beautiful cross, formed by transverse crevices in the big red peak. Again these crevices are filled with snow, and I am able to point out to Ida the marvellous cross, which apparently was the guide post for us all, and which we so appreciated on our first trip in 1934.

On and on we go, and I tell Ida how Stan met the boys at Virginia falls just a week ago, and transported them and all of their supplies in four round trips from the river just above the falls into Brintnell Lake. The Rabbit Kettle is off to our left. Mount Sydney Dobson, with its glacier-like crown, rears its mighty head, and directly underneath lie the blue waters of Brintnell Lake.

Here's the camp, pitched on the point just where I told them to place it, and above are the roaring cascades of the beautiful little creek which enters the lake at this point. With a wide sweep we are on the waters of the lake again, taxi-ing up. . . . What a welcome this is! Ted's meal is made up of soup, vegetables, a roast, bread, and of course, a pie.

We retire early after hearing the wonderful stories of the conquest of the river and the surveying work already done; also, that there are four nice big Billy Goats in the basin just above camp. This is most interesting, because it again settles the discussions whether any white mountain goats are to be found east of the Alaskan Coast range. Again the scientists are wrong . . . . Tomorrow we are going to fly north around the Snyder range, westwards, then south again . . . .

July 22: We circle twice over the lake in order to gain altitude and finally, at 6,000 feet, swing wide around the shoulder of the mountain and start up the Nahanni following the south fork. We can now see the snowfields of the Snyder range, and for the first time get a real idea of its gigantic size. Mile after mile it stretches away to the west, and at this eastern end is more than thirty miles wide. Peak after peak emerges from the surface of the snowfield, reaching up into clouds, and in each valley there is a long ribbon of ice . . . .

July 26: Fred Lambart, famous Alpinist, mountain man and geographer that he is, was most skeptical indeed when I first asked him to do the mapping and scientific work on this trip. Now that he has seen these mountains, be cannot sufficiently express his surprise, his amazement and delight at their sheer beauty. We have agreed that the survey job cannot be finished this year, but that it is of sufficient consequence to complete next year.

After dinner, while sitting round talking, admiring the surrounding landscape, we suddenly see Fred and his assistant Carl, at the very top of the "Colonel," the mountain forming the south buttress of the main range on the north shore of the lake. I get the big, 42-power glasses. We mount the glass on a tripod, and there they are putting up their proper flags, building the cairn, and we can even see them using their instruments. It is five minutes after six. They left camp this morning at seven o'clock. They have been eleven hours reaching the top. The "Colonel" proved to be 4,900 feet above the lake, which makes its total height 7,450 feet above sea level. Fred, even more than before, is delighted with the grandeur of the range and the magnitude of his task. This gives them four signal stations, and the base line, three miles long, has been properly measured, and now the real surveying work can start.

From "The Harry Snyder Canadian Expedition," by H. F. Lambart. <u>Canadian Alpine Journal</u> XXV (1937): 1-18.

I was privileged during the past summer, as a member of Mr. Harry Snyder's party, to visit the mountains, later named the Snyder Mountains by the Geographic Board of Canada, situated along the headwaters of the South Nahanni river, N.W.T., and to commence the very interesting work of making the first surveys of these mountains, which constitute a part of the main watershed separating the waters of the Yukon and Mackenzie rivers and which height of land constitutes the western boundary of the Northwest Territories.

The exploration and mapping of these mountains proved a very interesting task, our activities for this season being confined to the section in the neighborhood of Glacier lake. Here a geographical position was determined and a base and triangulation system laid out and measured, giving a good "ground control" and establishing in position and elevation all outstanding points visible from seven triangulation stations above the lake. The country thus covered represented about one hundred square miles.

No true elevations were known in the district so, by means of a battery of four aneroids transported and read by Air Pilot Stanley McMillan on his flights in and out of the country on July 15, 16, 24, 26, 27, 29 and 31, the elevations of three salient points were obtained, based on a sea elevation at Fort Simpson of 415 feet, which again derives its elevation from the only fixed sea level determination in the country, that at the end of the Sixth Meridian where it crosses the Mackenzie river 150 miles above Fort Simpson. . . .

The objective of the expedition was two-fold: the collection of biological specimens for the Museum of Natural History of New York and for the Victoria Museum at Ottawa, the chief interest being centered on obtaining specimens of the so-called "black-tailed sheep." All specimens were carefully collected under the competent supervision of Mr. George Goodwin,

Assistant Curator of Mammals of the American Museum of Natural History; and the mapping of the country, as far as that was possible in the time available during a very rainy season, which proved one of the worst on record.

The weather broke sufficiently for a few days in July and again towards the latter part of August permitting of the completion of the observations for latitude and longitude and azimuth, also the readings of horizontal and vertical angles from the high triangulation stations.

The results obtained appear to be highly satisfactory and the development of the map of the district is now being carried out with the use of photographs taken with infra-red plates, using the old type of government survey camera used in the days of the Alaska Boundary survey.

Mr. Snyder was anxious that entrance into the country should be made by the use of power boats ascending the South Nahanni river, which had grown old in romantic story and which is one of the most difficult in the entire Northwest Territories. The original intention was to gain entrance into Glacier lake by way of the South Nahanni river, and its tributary issuing from the lake.

A great deal of erroneous information had been given, as it later developed, and this would have been quite an impossible task, unless we had been willing to spend the entire summer cutting through long and tedious portages. Besides this, the difficult task of transporting the heavy poling boats over the mile and a quarter portage at Virginia falls would have had to be undertaken. Here there is a total rise of 473 feet to the highest point on the portage and then a drop of 80 feet to the slack water above the falls.

Some of the difficulties of the task of ascending the South Nahanni river may be gained from the following few statements of what actually happened:

The most difficult water on the river is confined to the section from "Hell's Gate" to the foot of Virginia falls. The drop here is something like twenty-one feet to the mile.

At Hell's Gate the river is confined to one narrow channel, its whole force striking against perpendicular walls on the right bank, turning a right angle and then doing the same sort of thing on the left bank, before again continuing on its normal course. One can imagine the water conditions in Hell's Gate itself: besides the very high "combers" and the "undertows" there is a periodic surge which makes the upstream passage particularly difficult, as we had good reason to know.

An old portage route exists around Hell's Gate, but George Roberts, who was employed at Fort Simpson, knew the river like a book and the decision was made to transport the loads of the two boats through by a number of light loads in Roberts' thirty-one-foot flat-bottom boat. This boat was made by Roberts of green, whip-sawn spruce and in spite of its unattractive appearance and flimsy construction, proved to be a splendid craft for these waters.

Karl Stein and I went up on the first load so that we could start on the measurements of Virginia falls and commence the arduous job of carrying our supplies over the portage to the slack water above the falls.

We got through Hell's Gate safely but it was a rough and exciting experience in this boat of Roberts' with two eight horse power Johnsons. The ten-mile run from here to the falls is a series of very swift rapids, which required very careful navigation. Finally, at 12:15 p.m. (2.45 hours' running time) from Hell's Gate, we rounded a point and there we came in sight of Virginia falls, the splendor of which simply beggars description. The water going over the falls was at normal stage, but even so the clouds of mist arising from the foot of the falls quite obscure the lower portion. They were first definitely recorded by Mr. Fenley Hunter when he saw them on August 22, 1928, naming them after his daughter.

A series of three base lines were measured on the south shore (left bank of the river) below the falls, and the height of the fall measured. The straight vertical fall is 300 feet. Niagara falls is 162 feet at its highest part so that the Virginia Falls is nearly twice as high as Niagara in vertical fall alone. Immediately above the falls there is a half mile of very steep rapids, referred to as the "sluice box." Here there is a total drop of ninety-three feet, thus making a total drop of 393 feet from slack water above the falls to the surface of the water immediately below....

A rough estimate of the flow was made. These calculations ... gave a total discharge of the South Nahanni river of 1200 foot-seconds. This would give an actual potential horse power at Virginia falls . . . of half a million horse power.

Fenley Hunter's account of his journey up the river in 1928 fills one with admiration. He worked his way up the 135 miles from the mouth to the foot of the falls with one small canoe driven by a light outboard motor. He speaks of having to line all the way from Hell's Gate to the falls. In this section as stated, the fall in the river is twenty-one feet to the mile. The total drop in the remaining 125 miles is about 1000 feet, which is equivalent to an average of eight feet to the mile.

SHORT HISTORIC SKETCH (for which I am indebted to Mr. Eric. S. Fry)

About 1900 an Indian named "Little Nahanni" brought a sample of rich gold bearing quartz into the mission at Fort Liard which he found near the mouth of the Flat river. In 1904 gold was found by an Indian from Telegraph creek on a stream entering the Flat river and a small stampede to the district started. Amongst those taking part in this rush was William McLeod of Fort Liard, who came out the following year with several ounces of what was reported to be coarse gold. McLeod, with his brother Frank and another man as partners, returned up the South Nahanni river in September 1905. Nothing having been heard of these men for some time, a search party entered the country in 1906 and found the bodies of the McLeod brothers in a camp on the lower Nahanni at a point now known as "Dead Man's Valley;" the third member of the party has never been heard of again.

A few years later, Poole Field, residing at the Ross River Post, received a letter from a prospector friend, one Jorgenson, telling him that he had made a rich strike. Field travelled over the divide with his dogs to the rendezvous indicated near the mouth of the Flat river only to find on arrival Jorgenson's headless body.

These happenings helped to keep the story of "The McLeod Mine" alive but for many years very little further investigation was carried out. A few years ago another prospector, Philip Powers, failed to return from a trip up the river and subsequently his charred remains were found with his burnt cabin.

In 1931 Jack Stanier, an old Yukon miner, and later a prospector in the Upper Liard District, heard rumors of a map being left by William McLeod with the mission at Fort Liard. This map, which was a very crude one, and to which no great importance had been attached, was with difficulty traced and with it Stanier proceeded up the South Nahanni river. In 1933 he found in a canyon on a creek, now shown on the map as McLeod creek, old workings and the remains of placer gold diggings. With this find Stanier came out certain that he had discovered the lost McLeod Mine. Newspapers then got the story into circulation, resulting in the entry of several parties into the country in 1933 and 1934 by dog team and aeroplane, who staked a number of claims and started a new development.

Gus Kraus from the Upper Hay River District, who came into the country with the later rush, remained skeptical over Stanier's find of the McLeod Brothers' mine. On this map two small lakes had been shown at the head of the creek in question. On Stanier Creek no such bodies of water were found. Kraus went exploring further afield and early in 1934 came on the upper waters of another creek which had two small lakes at its head. Gold was found on the upper branches and there he came upon old workings, sluice boxes, etc, all indicating that this was the McLeod mine. Present maps show this now as "Borden creek," renamed, however, by Kraus and his partner, as "Bennet creek," being the next creek above McLeod creek on the south side of the Flat river.

Stanier frankly admits now that his find, which started the rush in 1933-34, cannot be the McLeod Brothers' old workings and that Kraus has at last found the correct location.

To date this new field has hardly been scratched and may in the future be productive of rich mines. The formation is said to be entirely foreign to any of the country to the north and east, there being granite outcrops forming whole mountain ranges.

Thus, this story of the lure of gold has been the driving force in securing what we know of the South Nahanni river until very recent years.

We saw no natives in the country and scarcely a single evidence of their frequenting any of the valleys to any extent, though very old trails from east to west do exist crossing from the Yukon side over to the Mackenzie.

NARRATIVE

Our party consisted of George Goodwin, Assistant Curator of Mammals in the American Museum of Natural History, New York; Colonel A. J. McNab of Chicago; Karl Stein, who was to assist me in the field work; Jim Ross, outfitter of Hudson Hope on the Peace River, in charge of the party; Ted Boyton, cook, and Joe Callao, both from Hudson Hope, and myself -- making a total party of seven. . . .

The trip down the Slave river, through Great Slave lake, and then down the Mackenzie to Fort Simpson was uneventful. The delays experienced at ports of call seemed unwarranted and gave us no little concern, especially in this country where the summers are so pathetically short.

We arrived at Fort Simpson at 4:30 in the morning of June 30 and we were much impressed by its picturesque setting on the top of a high bank commanding a view of the Mackenzie river and just below the wide mouth of the Liard river with its few wooded islands so lavishly covered with greenery. The whole outlook is one of the most beautiful along the river. It is a busy little centre with an Indian agency, a well-equipped hospital, Anglican and Roman Catholic churches, a wireless station and very fine Hudson Bay buildings, besides the buildings of a few other traders. The whole water front scene is particularly attractive with gardens -- a profusion of flowers, which were of particular interest and pleasure.

Here at Fort Simpson the serious work of the summer commenced. We went into camp in a sheltered cove above town and proceeded to get stores properly in order and much equipment properly straightened out. The small sponson canoe was left behind and in its place a splendid thirty-one-foot pointer boat with outboard was taken. Its owner, George Roberts, was also employed here; he was an experienced river man and thoroughly familiar with the South Nahanni river waters. Roberts' services proved invaluable. Thursday, July 1, found us all packed up in the morning ready for the journey planned to ascend the Liard river and thence up the South Nahanni river.

In a very few minutes we were out of the Mackenzie river and entered the mouth of the Liard river. Not far up Roberts' engine broke a crank shaft and it was decided to camp while Roberts went back to Simpson for engine repairs. The next day Roberts returned and we continued on our way and in 5.43 hours' running time came to the "Beaver Dam," the foot of the fifteen-mile rapids of the Liard river. With plenty of daylight at this time of year and these rapids to ascend, Jim Ross wisely decided to push on, so we continued, just struggling along and negotiating some very difficult corners along the left bank. We stopped at midnight for tea and at 4:30 a.m. of July 3 emerged from the rapids and stopped for a very welcome rest and a good breakfast in a sheltered cove just above the last of the swift water. The stage of water was high, but I would not say in flood although the "Beaver Dam" was well submerged. We passed the Hudson's Bay steamer, the Deas Lake, pushing a scow and moving very slowly, just opposite St. Mary's island at the head of the rapid.

We were anxious to get through to Nahanni Forks so we pushed on throughout the day, enjoying very much the river and the wide open expanses, and then the coming into view of the bold limestone mountains along the northwestern horizon some twenty miles back. Flat open country skirts both shores of the Liard, then finally we caught glimpses of that lovely group of hills culminating in the Nahanni Butte at the mouth of the Nahanni river. At 9:00 p.m. we arrived at Nahanni Forks -- twenty-six running hours from Fort Simpson.

We were glad to pull out of this miserable tumbledown, mosquito-infested place at 1:45 p.m. the next day, Sunday, July 4, and to commence the ascent of the South Nahanni river with somewhat reduced loads and a fresh supply of gasoline, for which we paid dearly.

The lower Nahanni valley, to start with, is low and well wooded, and then the river breaks up into innumerable channels and spreads out over a very wide valley. Soon the river narrows again and we found low limestone ridges cut through by the river, and ahead the country rises rapidly but smoothly on tilted beds of limestone; the river breaks its way through these magnificent box-like canyons.

We arrived at the foot of this first canyon at noon on the 6th, being a run of nineteen hours from the mouth of the river. Here the famous hot springs are located, consisting of numerous sulphurous springs in the form of a series of pot holes, all joined by small tributary streams in the midst of a timber growth, with some small meadows covering an area of not more than a mile square. The temperature of the water was measured and found to be ninety-five degrees Fahrenheit. There were no unusual forms of flora or timber present, and strange to say, there seemed to be an unusual absence of game trails.

The next day was occupied in running up the first canyon, making its total length of sixteen miles in 6.50 hours actual running time. In the canyons, the water is generally in the one channel and the navigation fairly easy with lots of water. Near the head of this first canyon there are two difficult rapids through which navigation was difficult with the large boat.

The next morning was spent running through what is known as "Dead Man's valley," and then we entered the second canyon with its high cliffs of rock and mountain ridges rising to 2500 feet above the water. The upper end of the "Little valley" between the second and third canyons was reached in the late afternoon where we camped for the night. Heavy rains delayed us the next day until the afternoon, when we managed, however, to get on our way again and make the short run to "The Gate." Here we were ninety-eight miles from the forks of the Nahanni, which had taken 38.2 hours to run.

"The Gate" is an inspiring sight, being in a perfect hair-pin bend of the river where it has cut its way through vertical cliffs 700 feet high (measured). The channel of the river in the centre of "The Gate" is 250 feet wide. In a camp site just above, commanding a magnificent view through "The Gate," we spent the night. This camp was occupied by Mr. Snyder and his party when they first ascended this river in 1935. Here around "The Gate" and up the river to the Mary river is the sheep country we are to visit on our way out in the autumn and where the specimens of the black-tailed sheep were obtained.

The next day, Saturday the 10th, we continued on our way, making a point three miles below the mouth of the Flat river at 7:30 p.m. We passed the mouth of Mary river at 4:20 p.m., which marks the end of the bold high relief which gives way to a lower plateau type of country cut by streams, with wide open valleys and isolated miniature groups of mountain ranges. The characteristic structure of limestone canyons has gone, and in its place a country more inviting in appearance with a more abundant timber growth exists. The valley of the Flat river, as seen from the mouth, is open and one gets an impression of a great expanse of country beyond.

Looking up the South Nahanni river from the mouth of the Flat there are rolling, heavily eroded smooth ridges with an occasional sugar-loaf type of relief which is very pleasing to the eye. The side hills are soft and delicately timbered with poplar and small birch, with a scattering of evergreens. From the water, as we passed along, a deep game trail was seen coming down to the river from the elevated plateaus. This day's run of only 4.05 hours when we passed the mouth of the Flat river, was a very short one, having been forced into camp just opposite the mouth of Wrigley creek as a result of a serious accident to our large motor. For no apparent reason the main lower shaft suddenly gave way in a concentric cone break. In a sense this was providential as here we were situated just below the worst stretches of the whole river and a very short distance below "Hell's Gate," the most dangerous part of the entire river and already described in my opening remarks. By necessity, the large boat was left behind and the contents of the two boats relayed up the remaining ten miles to the foot of Virginia falls in a series of light loads in the smaller boat. As previously stated, this ten-mile section is the most difficult on the river and a very fine piece of work was accomplished in landing all our supplies safely at the foot of the falls three days later, Wednesday, July 14. Three of the party walked the distance from a camp three miles below the foot of the falls to our camp at the slack water above the falls.

During the period of relaying on the river, Karl and I had finished our survey of the falls and had portaged a goodly proportion of the provisions and equipment around the falls, so, when Stan McMillan arived with the Fairchild's on Thursday, July 15, we were all ready to be off by air for the seventy-mile journey to Glacier lake -- the central point of our operations for the summer. The third and last load left at 6 p.m. and by night our camp was completely installed on a splendid timbered delta at the upper end of this lake.

One never becomes quite accustomed to these sudden changes, due to this comparatively new means of transport, after years of laborious travel by pack-train and every other primitive means of transportation, to be suddenly taken aloft and carried by air will always remain a marvel to me.

An entirely new country lay before us, untouched by anyone, to deal with as best we could. To George Goodwin fell the task of collecting its fauna, and I, after first determining its proper place upon the earth's surface, was to commence a systematic survey, and place in position its outstanding geographical features to serve as a fundamental control system, and then to knit together all these in the production of a topographical map as far as the time and the weather would permit.

With my mind centered on this work, we made all progress possible until the day of our departure, when the plane came in for us and we were taken out on August 31.

The weather conditions in the country were very bad this year, but the work as above outlined progressed continuously, with the exception of a very pleasant intermission when Mr. and Mrs. Snyder came in to be with us for ten days, from July 21, being flown in by Stan McMillan and Archie Vanhee, mechanic . . . .

We know much of the relief and the character of the mountains in the vicinity of Glacier lake, and that they are of igneous origin and very young in geological origin.

A point we called "The Cathedral," at the west end of the lake, is of unbroken gray granite. Within less than two miles of this peak a stream has deposited on the rocks a crust of iron rust which, when broken off, proved to be four inches thick. So there is here a great admixture of limestone, shale and slate, ferric rocks and granite. The highest elevation so far determined is 9045 feet, but I have no doubt that higher peaks will be found in the region as the surveys are extended, and which Mr. Snyder hopes to do this coming summer. . . .

Our initial observation station, East base and West base were very carefully and permanently marked on the ground by large boulders which were sunk flush with the ground and a bronze tablet cemented into a drilled hole. Of the seven triangulation stations established, five were climbed twice, our highest climbs being over 5000 feet above the lake. The triangulation points also constitute camera stations, so that we have material now on hand to plot a fair-sized togographical map of the region. It was felt that the triangulation control of the region was of very great value where none such existed within many miles, and this becomes doubly true if, by the use of aerial photographs, attempts are made to cover all the country of high relief with aerial photographs.

When Mr. and Mrs. Snyder left on July 21 to fly out to keep an engagement with His Excellency, the Governor General [eds-Lord Tweedsmuir], at the Eldorado Mine on Great Bear lake, they took George Roberts with them and left him at Virginia falls with instructions to take the large boat down river to some point where it could be handled by our party coming out later and who would be obliged to navigate the river in it with one of the smaller engines. This Roberts accomplished successfully alone, leaving the boat in a section of the river about eight miles below the mouth of the Flat river, where it was plainly visible from the air.

When Stanley McMillan came in for us on August 29, the plan next day was to completely evacuate our lovely camp on the shores of Glacier Lake, leaving behind but very few articles. These could very well be left there until the next year, amongst which was the canoe which was constructed so as to be taken apart in four sections, and which had proved so indispensable on the lake.

After landing five of the party, and all their outfit, at the boat anchored by Roberts eight miles below the mouth of the Flat river, Stan returned to take George Goodwin and Colonel

McNab out to Fort Simpson, where they subsequently obtained air transportation to the outside.

The party of five of us, left on the banks of the river below the mouth of Flat river, went into camp near the mouth of Mary river, and commenced a very enjoyable but arduous ten days' hunting of the "black-tailed sheep."

The ranges of these sheep are along the summits of the long flat ridges 2500 to 3000 feet above the river valley above and below "The Gate." In this section of country the gulches are well timbered but the tops are open alplands covered, in many of the lower and more sheltered sections, with quite a heavy growth of brush which, I am disposed to think, furnishes much of their winter shelter and no doubt fodder. We camped at the mouth of the Mary river, at "The Gate," and at a point a few miles below and, in our excursions abroad, covered a large stretch of country besides what we were able to cover with field glasses, from high points of vantage. The specimens collected were carefully chosen and were for the museums at Ottawa and New York.

Our swift return down the South Nahanni river was a very easy and very pleasant one, under magnificent weather conditions and the shores decked in their most gorgeous autumn tinting.

"Botanical Exploration of the Mackenzie Mountains" by Hugh M. Raup. <u>Arnold Arboretum Bulletin of Popular Information</u>, Ser.4, VII. 13 (15 December 1939): 69-71.

The Arnold Arboretum as part of its general program of field work sponsored a collecting expedition to the Mackenzie Mountains during the past summer. The main objectives were to make collections representing the flora of a part of this unknown region, and a study of the local types of vegetation. The net results will be a contribution to the broader problems of boreal phytogeography, for the summer's work will throw light on one of the largest blank spots in our plant maps of the northern part of the continent. The field work was in charge of the writer, who, with his wife, had been engaged in the botanical investigation of the Mackenzie basin for several years; and was financed in part by grants from the Milton Fund of Harvard University, the American Academy of Arts and Sciences, and the National Academy of Science. The National Museum of Canada made generous loans of field equipment. Mr. James H. Soper, of Hamilton, Ontario, served as field assistant. Since it was especially desirable to reach the mountains for spring collecting (mid-June), and since the Mackenzie system at Great Slave Lake is not commonly open to navigation so early in the season, plans for the whole trip had to be made a year ahead of time. Most of the food supplies, collecting outfit, and heavier camping equipment were packed and shipped to the Hudson's Bay Company at Fort Simpson in the summer of 1938. The party left Boston May 20, 1939, and reached Simpson on June 8th, using a Mackenzie Air Service plane for the last and ordinarily most time-consuming stage of the journey -- north from Fort Smith. A week at Simpson gave time to sort and re-pack supplies, and to collect the local spring flora along the Mackenzie River.

On the 16th a chartered plane carried us to Brintnell Lake, a small body of water at an altitude of 2600 feet in the Snyder Range, approximately 200 miles west of Fort Simpson. This range lies in the heart of the Mackenzie Mountain system, and is composed of rugged granite and shale mountains, some of which reach elevations 9000 feet or more above the sea.

It would be difficult to conceive of a more completely primeval country than this. Two years ago a surveying party sponsored by Mr. Harry Snyder of Montreal (for whom the mountains were named) camped there for a few weeks; and trappers spent a winter on the lake a few years ago. Aside from these few visitors the lake and its surrounding mountains seem never to have been inhabited by human beings. No evidence of Indian occupation could be found. Overland travel proved extremely difficult due to the steep slopes and the complete absence of man-made trails.

The flora is a small one in number of species, and strongly Arctic in character. Nevertheless a remarkably rich forest of spruce grows on the lower slopes of the mountains. The timber line is from 1200 to 1400 feet above the lake, with colorful alpine meadow and crevice vegetation above. The steeper slopes everywhere are made difficult for plant growth by the prevalence of hazardous slide-rock; and on the steep southward-facing surfaces the vegetation is subject to great damage by periodic spring snow-slides. Collecting and field studies of local distribution problems engaged our attention until another plane came for us on the 20th of August. A sectional canoe made possible short trips about the lake, but otherwise we went on foot to the surrounding country. No two mountain slopes had the same flora, so that the collecting did not become monotonous in spite of our confinement to one region. . . .

The summer's collecting netted some 15,000 herbarium specimens, over two thirds of which are of flowering plants and ferns, and the remainder lichens, mosses and fungi . . . . The collections will be studied at the Arboretum and the duplicates distributed from it in exchange with herbaria throughout the world.

Excerpts from <u>The Botany of Southwestern Mackenzie</u>, by Hugh M. Raup. Published by the Arnold Arboretum of Harvard University in <u>Sargentia</u> VI, 28 February 1947.

[Editors' note: Raup wrote this book as a professional biologist writing for biologists. We have modified his text for the general reader, indicating omissions by the use of ellipses, and additions by the use of square brackets. Scientific (Latin) plant names were replaced by common (English) names where available. Raup's lengthy lists of secondary species for each plant community were omitted. Visitors to the lake who wish to follow Raup's researches in any detail will need the full text, available in major academic libraries, as well as a contemporary source of color photos of plants, such as Lone Pine's <u>Plants of Northern British Columbia</u>]

INTRODUCTION AND ACKNOWLEDGMENTS

The broad outlines of the botany of boreal America began to take form in the first half of the nineteenth century, particularly in the works of Sir John Richardson and William Hooker. Not since that time, with the exception of John Macoun's "Catalogue of Canadian Plants," have any attempts been made to prepare general descriptions either of the flora or of the botanical landscapes. . . .

It was to be expected that more intensive study should be subdivided on a geographic basis. The present paper deals with one of these geographical areas, in the southwestern part of the District of Mackenzie (Northwest Territories), and may be divided roughly into four parts. The first is a general description of the region . . . . Second is an account of the plant communities that together form the botanical aspects of the landscapes. . . . Third is a study of the geographic affinities of some species and communities. . . . Finally there is an annotated catalogue of . . . vascular plants.

The area treated in this paper is bounded on the west and south by the borders between the District of Mackenzie, Yukon, British Columbia, and Alberta. On the east it extends to the Slave River, Great Slave Lake, and Marian River. Its northern boundary is approximately at lat. 64 degrees 30', making the northern limit on the Mackenzie River a short distance above Norman. . . .

The Great Bear Lake and lower Mackenzie regions will be treated by A. E. Porsild in his forthcoming <u>Flora of the Northwest Territories</u> . . . Botanical investigations in the areas to the south and southeast have been reported upon in some of my own papers [dated from 1930 to 1945], while the region of the Alaska Highway in northern British Columbia will be the subject of papers growing out of [my] field work of 1943 and 1944. The flora of the Yukon is being studied and published upon at the present time by Dr. Eric Hultén.

Mackenzie Air Service Ballanca drops the Raup Expedition at the west end of Glacier Lake. Pilot R.C. (Bob) Randall.

The material basis for the present studies is principally in three collections. The first was made by Dr. James H. Soper and myself at Fort Simpson and at Brintnell [Glacier] Lake in the Mackenzie Mountains during the summer of 1939. The second is a collection made by A. E. Porsild on the eastern slopes of the Mackenzie Mountains along the Canol Road in the autumn of

77

1944, and the third was made by Dr. V.C. Wynne-Edwards of McGill University in the same area during the summer of 1944. . . . Also I have examined numerous duplicates from the Richardson collections made at the time of the first and second Franklin Expeditions and now to be found in the herbaria at the New York Botanical Garden, Harvard University, and the National Museum of Canada. . . .

It is impossible to mention individually all the people who helped to forward the field work. Mr. Harry Snyder of Montreal placed at our disposal indispensable information about the Brintnell lake country, with copies of the manuscript map of the lake and its environs made during his expedition of 1937. Officials of the Hudson's Bay Company and the Mackenzie Air Service were, as usual, most helpful in organizing our supplies and transportation. It is impossible to express too great appreciation of the kindness and hospitality of our many friends at Fort Simpson . . . . Special thanks are due to Archdeacon and Mrs. Harry G. Cook, who took us into their home, and to Capt. George Isbister who was in charge of the Government Radio Station.

Finally it is a pleasure to express my obligation to my wife and to Dr. James H. Soper, field companions of the expedition of 1939. Without their unfailing patience, enthusiasm, and good will, the measure of success achieved would have been impossible.

THE TOPOGRAPHY OF SOUTHWESTERN MACKENZIE

The most prominent topographic feature of southwestern Mackenzie is formed by the Mackenzie Mountains, which lie along its western border. These mountains appear to be a part of the Rocky Mountain system, but their central axis is displaced eastward from that of the latter. . . .

The Mackenzie Mountain system begins at the Liard River and extends in a northwesterly direction in a great arc some 600 miles long. According to Camsell, it covers an area of 75,000 to 100,000 square miles and is regarded as the largest mountain group in Canada. Keele's description (1910) made as he crossed the range from west to east by way of the Ross and Gravel Rivers, will serve to characterize the topography.

"The mountains as seen from the west present a massive and continuous front, unbroken by lowland areas. The crestline is uneven in profile, however, and the course of the ranges varies, with subdued types of mountains among the more rugged ones. The structure is characterized by folding on a broad scale, with the folds sometimes close-set or overthrust. The western slopes are trenched by wide valleys that cut well back to the divide.... The higher and more rugged mountains are granite stocks which have resisted weathering much better than the intervening sedimentary rocks. Glacial erosion and deposit have greatly modified the surface features, smoothing the bedrock and strewing the valley floors and lower slopes with drift and outwash. In this western part of the range the mountains are commonly over 7000 feet high, and a few reach 9000 feet.

"About forty miles east of the divide the topography changes ... and a more compact and rugged mountain region is entered. The drainage channels in this region are confined in narrow valleys, with steep, barren slopes of rock and talus, the rivers in the bottom flowing in a very contracted bed, which at rare intervals opens out into a narrow alluvial flat.

"The structure of these mountains differs from that of the ranges to the west, being apparently due to fracturing, buckling and faulting of the strata, and the residual masses present the appearance of a series of faulted and tilted blocks. The principal lines of fracture are in a northwest-southeast direction, and the beds have a prevailing southwesterly dip.

"The Mackenzie mountains, as a whole, have a maximum width of about 300 miles . . . Both in geology and structure the eastern portion of these mountains is closely related to the Rocky mountains in southern Canada.

A portion of the drainage of the western slope of the Mackenzie mountains falls into the Frances river, and thence by the Liard and Mackenzie rivers into the Beaufort Sea, but the greater part is taken by tributaries of the Yukon river to the Bering Sea. All the drainage of the eastern slope falls into the Mackenzie River. . . .

"Owing to the great difference in precipitation the streams from the west side of the divide carry down to the Yukon more than twice as much water as the streams over an equal area on the eastern side. . . ."

Lucy and Karl, collecting lichen.

The maximum height attained by the Mackenzie Mountains is as yet unknown. A granite peak at Brintnell lake has been estimated with reasonable accuracy at about 8500 feet, while still higher elevations have been reported between there and the Gravel River.

The first white men to visit southwestern Mackenzie were those in Alexander Mackenzie's exploring party of 1798. The narrative of this expedition gives the course of the Slave and Mackenzie Rivers, outlines parts of the northwest shore of Great Slave Lake, and gives the approximate position of the Caribou, Horn, Eagle, Mackenzie, and Richardson Mountains. It is filled with observations on the plant and animal life of the region, as well as on the life of the aborigines. Mackenzie's voyage was designed to open the country for the fur trade, and the great river soon became the principal highway in this trade and the scene of its permanent establishments. No doubt a certain amount of explorations away from the main route was carried on by the traders, but no account of it is available. Even the explorations of Sir John Franklin and his parties (1823, 1828), which made such outstanding contributions to the geography of the northwest, added little to the knowledge of our region. They passed through it only as Mackenzie did, by way of the main river.

Attempts to use the Liard River as a trade route into the Cassiar region and the upper Yukon proved futile, due to the difficulties of navigation. Part of the upper Liard country was visited by the Hudson's Bay Company trader Robert Campbell, who traveled down the Dease and up the Liard and Frances Rivers to Frances Lake in 1840. . . .

More accurate descriptions of the surface features and geology of our region began to take form for the first time in the reports published by the Geological Survey and the Department of Interior of Canada in 1888, 1890, and 1891. These reports were based upon a series of remarkable survey journeys made in 1887 and 1888 by G. M. Dawson (1888), R. G. McConnell (1891) and William Ogilvie (1890). . . . As a result of these three expeditions the Mackenzie River was more accurately mapped, the Liard was surveyed for the first time up as far as the Frances, and the configuration of the Mackenzie Mountain mass began to appear in its true form. Also the broad outlines of the geology of the region were formulated. All of the reports are filled with pertinent notes on the vegetation and its distribution - particularly the report of Dawson, who was one of the most discerning naturalists ever to visit the Northwest. . . .

A crossing of the Mackenzie mountains was first described by Joseph Keele, of the Canadian Geological Survey . . . . In the summer of 1907 Keele made a reconnaissance survey along the Pelly up to about 140 miles above its junction with the Ross River. He then ascended the Ross to its headwaters, where he found a mountain pass to the head of the Gravel River, which he descended to the Mackenzie. The journey through the mountains required the entire winter and spring of 1907 - 08. Keele's report is a mine of first-hand information on the topography, climate, flora, fauna, Indians, and geological structure of the Mackenzie Mountains. Until very recently it was the only source of data on this little-known wilderness. I have drawn upon it frequently and at length during our field work of 1939 and in the preparation of the present paper. . . .

Dr. Charles Camsell (1936) . . . flew eastward over the plateau region of the upper Liard, and down to the Mackenzie. His brief paper describing the flight contains some excellent photographs and an account of the geography of this unexplored wilderness as seen from the air. . . . In 1937 Mr. Harry Snyder of Montreal took a survey party to Brintnell Lake (shown on some maps as Glacier Lake), a small body of water near the head of the South Nahanni River. . . . Accompanying Mr. Snyder were Dr. George Goodwin, a zoologist from the American Museum of Natural History, and Mr. Fred Lambart, a surveyor. Triangulation points were set up on the lake shores, and a topographic map was made of the lake and of the mountains immediately surrounding it. This map was used to good advantage by our party in 1939 . . . .

The Arnold Arboretum expedition of 1939 reached Fort Simpson on June 8, traveling by the usual steamer route from Waterways to Fitzgerald, and by air from Fort Smith to

Simpson. Supplies had been shipped to Simpson in the preceding year. After about a week of collecting at Simpson, the party, equipment, and supplies were flown to Brintnell Lake in a chartered Mackenzie Air Service plane. We remained at the lake until the 20th of August, making collections of the flora and records of its local distribution and the structure of plant communities. Three weeks were then spent at Simpson, making further collections. . . .

GEOLOGY AND SOILS

Most of the rocks exposed in the Mackenzie Mountains are sediments of Paleozoic age . . . . The western part of the range has been intruded by masses of granite that form the cores of the higher and more rugged mountains. . . . Further south these intrusions form the so-called Snyder Range, west of the upper South Nahanni. Being much harder than the surrounding sediments they have weathered into serrated ridges which stand out conspicuously among the other mountain summits of the region. . . .

Glacial ice in the Mackenzie Mountains was thought by Keele to have been confluent with the Cordilleran ice mass of the Rocky Mountains, and to have had its gathering ground on the western slopes of the range. He estimated its thickness in the Ross River region at about 3000 feet, which would mean that it did not cover the higher peaks. He states that "the movement of the ice . . . was controlled to a great extent by the main drainage valleys, and flowed down those almost, but not quite, to the Yukon River." It is of further note that Keele thought the ice divide shifted from west to east. He found granite from the western slopes far down the eastern side of the range . . .

The exact relationship between the two glacial systems at the eastern front of the Mackenzie Mountains is yet to be worked out.

Brintnell Lake . . . is about 3 1/4 miles long and about half a mile wide at its widest point. The trend of its main axis is approximately W. 20 degrees N., while the position of its western end is about in latitude 62 degrees 5' N. and longitude 127 degrees 35' W. Its altitude is about 2600 feet above sea level. The bottom has not yet been found, but it is evidently quite deep. Mr. Harry Snyder . . . informed me that he put down about 1000 feet of cable without reaching bottom. The lake is held to its present level by a rock barrier at the eastern end, through which the outflowing stream pours in a narrow, unnavigable gorge. This stream joins the South Nahanni about 5 miles down the valley and perhaps 800 or 1000 feet below the lake.

The mountains rise steeply from the north and south shores to heights of 6000 to 7000 feet above sea-level. About two miles west of the lake there is a higher peak that attains an elevation of approximately 8500 feet. Several streams feed the lake from the neighboring slopes, but the main intake is from a creek which flows through a great U-shaped valley to the west. This creek is fed by glaciers in the high mountains at the head of the valley about 7 miles above the lake. The valley floor west of the lake is made up of gravel plains and broad marshy flats of light-colored glacial clay. When our party arrived on June 16 the lake water was nearly clear, but within a few days it became "milky" from glacial melt water and remained so throughout the summer.

The mountain rocks immediately surrounding the lake are Paleozoic shales and slates. The higher peaks to the west and north, however, are composed of light-colored granites which produce jagged, serrate profiles. The contact between granites and sediments is clearly seen where it angles up the side of a mountain just west of the lake. The presence of granite peaks in the upper South Nahanni country was not known until quite recently. In terms of Keele's division of the Mackenzie range into eastern and western phases, this region should be placed with the western section, where intrusive granites form the cores of the higher mountains. . . .

The contrast between the topography and soils of the shale and granite areas is striking. A small stream, Frost Creek, entering the north side of the lake near the western end, issues from a hanging valley in the shale mountains. The lower end, or rather the rim, of this valley is about 1400 feet above the lake. From various points in the valley and on its lateral slopes there are good views of the higher topography formed from this kind of rock. In spite of the steep dip of the strata, many of the upper slopes have become rounded and have produced through weathering a fair amount of soil. Below the summits, however, there are large areas of slide rock, much of which is still in motion, forming great "rivers" of rock down the slopes and in the higher gullies. The degree of stability in this slide rock determines, and is in turn conditioned by, the amount of vegetation growing on it. North slopes are of course cliff-like and at the higher elevations are almost completely devoid of vegetation. The talus here is so active that plants can hardly get a footing. By contrast the country a little farther west, where the granite peaks rise out of the shales, shows very little soil produced in situ. The granite cores are exfoliating in enormous blocks and slabs to form ponderous and almost sterile talus slopes. The granite peaks show almost no green plant life.

The break-up of the mountain rocks and the formation of talus is going on continuously and rapidly. While we were camped at the lake we frequently heard the rumbling sound of landslides, and occasionally we saw clouds of dust rising from the high slopes or caught sight of huge blocks of stone as they tumbled off the cliffs and bounced to a standstill on the talus. Conspicuous features of the lake shores are points formed by steep fans of rock debris. These are most highly developed on the north shore at the foot of the precipitous north slope of Colonel Mountain. . . .

The glacier at the head of the main stream is obviously the remnant of a larger one which once flowed down the lake valley. The U-shaped form of the valley, with its sharply truncated transverse ridges, is clear evidence of this. The truncated slopes have a gradient of about 34 degrees from the horizontal and descend into the lake with scarcely any shore formation. All of the fans mentioned above postdate the retreat of the ice.

Glacial deposits were found up to an altitude of approximately 4000 feet in the main valley and 5000 feet in the valley of Frost Creek. In the main valley they are of two kinds. On the south-facing slopes north of the lake are ridges of gravel and boulder clay festooned diagonally down the steep slopes in a south-easterly direction. The channels of the streams cutting through the ridges are filled with boulders from the till. These deposits are rather loose and uncompacted, with little or no evidence of cementing. On the opposite side of the lake, masses of till were found packed into the great gullies on the north slope of Colonel Mountain, indicating that the gullies and intervening hogbacks were formed before the last advance of the glacier. Presumably the till completely filled the gullies to a height of about 4000 feet, at which level the remains of it form shoulders on the truncated fronts of the hogbacks. The fact that these shoulders have truncated surfaces which are confluent with those of the underlying rocks of the hogbacks indicates that this till antedates the last advance of the ice and must have been deposited during an older advance and retreat. . . .

North of the lake, in the hanging valley mentioned above, are tills which form terraces on the valley slopes. The highest of these terraces is at about 5000 feet, near the rim of the valley, and is composed of unsorted drift in which the boulders are principally of granite. Large erratic boulders are frequent on the surface. There are at least two sets of terraces, representing two periods of stream dissection through the drift. The lower is of very loose gravelly till, also made up principally of granite stones.

There is therefore unmistakable evidence of two advances and retreats of a glacier in the main lake valley . . . . The character of the rocks in the older till of the main valley suggests that they came from the western slopes of the Mackenzie range. . . . The prevalence of granites in the younger tills suggests that the center of the spread for the main ice mass may have shifted eastward, as Keele thought it did. The absence of western rocks in the drift of the hanging valley might well be due to its local origin as a tributary glacier among the granite mountains immediately north of the lake. . . .

The influence of frost upon the formation and movement of soils is everywhere to be seen. Well-defined stone rings were found in a springy area on the till in the upper valley of Frost Creek. The rings range in diameter from a few inches to six feet or more. Many of the upper mountain slopes are literally covered with turf-banked terraces in varying stages of stabilization. The rounded contours of many of the higher slopes on the shale mountains appear to be due to long-continued soil formation and solifluction caused by Glacial period, as it is very probable that summits above 5000 feet were not covered by glaciers. Similar topography is to be seen on many mountains in the South Nahanni country, as well as along the Canol Road.

CLIMATE AND AGRICULTURE

I shall limit this treatment . . . to a brief and general characterization of the climate of the region of Fort Simpson, and I shall attempt to draw up some contrasts between the climate of Simpson and that of the Brintnell Lake district. The principal sources of published information for the vicinity of Simpson are in papers by McConnell (1981), Preble (1908), Kindle (1920) and Albright (1933, 1937).

Warm weather begins in spring during late April or early May. In 1888 McConnell reported that the temperature rose above freezing for the first time on April 20, and after May 1 the snow rapidly disappeared . . . .

The ice in the Liard River breaks up in spring before that of the Mackenzie. In 1904 this occurred on April 29. The Liard ice drove a channel across the Mackenzie and piled up high on the north bank. The breakup of the Mackenzie ice below the Liard did not occur until May 2. [Kindle states] that the average dates of opening at Simpson are between May 10 and 15.

The Mackenzie ice does not open between Great Slave Lake and Simpson until two and a half or three weeks after the ice has gone out below the latter place. Great Slave lake itself usually opens between June 16 and July 2.

In the autumn the larger bays of Great Slave Lake become covered with ice in October, early or late, depending upon the season. In the wider parts of the lake the water may remain open until mid-November. The upper Mackenzie usually closes in the latter half of November, though it is sometimes closed to canoe navigation in mid-October. In terms of vegetation growth, the season ends during the latter half of August or early in September. Most of the native flora has set its fruit by the last week in August.

At the time of our arrival in Simpson on June 8, 1939, the spring was far advanced. About fifty species of plants were found in flower there during the week between June 9 and June 16. We experienced the first frost at Simpson on August 24, soon after our return there from Brintnell Lake. . . . The first killing frost has sometimes been reported quite late. Albright states that it did not occur in 1930 until September 24, and Kindle recorded the first notable freeze in 1920 on September 25.

Successful gardens have been grown at Simpson for many years. Root crops, such as potatoes, carrots, and rutabagas, are particularly successful, and some oats and barley are raised. Squaw corn will not mature, but will produce roasting ears. Vegetable marrow is raised from seed, and tomatoes will occasionally ripen out of doors. Most tomatoes are taken in to ripen, however, for it is estimated that they will ripen on the vine in only about two years in ten.

Approximately fifty acres are under cultivation, mostly on the island, but in part on a low flood plain on the west bank of the river. No cultivation has been attempted except on the alluvial soils along the main river. Domestic livestock is wintered successfully, supplementing the feed with wild hay cut in the neighborhood. Some of his hay comes from the semi-open prairies on the upland west of the river. Of crops raised in excess of local needs, potatoes and rutabagas are most important. They are shipped down the river to missions where gardening is not so profitable.

COMPARISON OF THE CLIMATES OF SIMPSON AND BRINT-NELL LAKE

Our party spent 61 days at Brintnell between June 16 and August 20. During this period 60 maximum and minimum temperatures were recorded [in Fahrenheit] with a Sixes type thermomenter placed in a protected situation on the shore of the lake about four feet above the ground. The altitude of Simpson is approximately 420 feet above sea-level, and that of the lake about 2600 feet.

Average maximum, 72.8 at Simpson, 65.7 at Brintnell L. Absolute maximum temperature 84.0 at Simpson, 83.5 at Brintnell. Average minimum temperature, 48.6 at Simpson, 43.6 at Brintnell. Absolute minumum temperature, 36 at Simpson, 32 at Brintnell. No. of days 60 degrees or below, 4 at Simpson, 13 at Brintnell. . . . No. of days on which rain fell, 19 at Simpson, 19 at Brintnell. No. of clear or partly cloudy days, 54 at Simpson, 41 at Brintnell. . . . Periods of storminess were somewhat more numerous at the lake.

PLANT COMMUNITIES IN THE BRINTNELL LAKE AREA

The most prominent plant communities in the vicinity of Brintnell Lake in the Mackenzie Mountains are the forests of the lower mountain slopes, a sub-alpine scrub zone made up principally of willows and dwarf birch on the middle slopes, and a varied group of tundra [alpine] communities at higher levels. Timber line is between 3800 and 5000 feet above sea-level, or 1200 to 2400 feet above the lake. The subalpine scrub varies greatly in vertical width, but in places covers nearly 1000 feet. Timber lines on the north- and south-facing slopes in some places differ but little in elevation, although the character of the forests is quite different.

As stated elsewhere, most of the shores of the lake are precipitous, so that space for the development of communities other than those just mentioned is limited. A few small muskegs have developed, chiefly at the eastern and western ends of the lake, while in the valley of the glacial stream that enters from the west are deposits of mud upon which a marsh type of vegetation appears. The lowland along this stream also contains some gravel and sand bars that have produced characteristic communities. Large fans composed of stones and gravel occur at several places around the lake, to produce the nearest approach to beaches that the area affords.

Forests

The most mesophytic forests at Brintnell Lake are situated on the lower slopes of the mountains, extending only a few hundred feet above the level of the lake:

[The Lower Forests]

PRIMARY SPECIES. Trees: white spruce var. albertiana. Shrubs: paper birch var. *commutata, betula papyrifera* var. *humilis*, green alder, red swamp currant, rose hip, soapberry, highbush cranberry. Ground: brown moss spp., *Peltigera aphthosa* [freckled lichen], lingenberry var. *minus*.

The spruces commonly attain breast-height diameters of 2-3 feet and heights of 60 - 100 feet. The mat of mosses and duff in the oldest forest observed was at least 15 inches thick. The mineral substratum is usually very rough, composed principally of the larger talus rocks that have reached the lower slopes and the coarser materials of the upper parts of the alluvial fans. On sites that have not been altered by fire the heavy mat of mosses completely covers all but the largest boulders. In spite of their excellent diameter and height growth, most of the trees on the slopes have much twisted grain and a large amount of compression wood on their down-hill sides near the base. Nearly all are bent to their vertical positions from near the base, indicating that they have suffered from land-slip, or snow-slides, or both. The shrub layer is not dense, and offers but little hindrance to travel through the woods. The principal difficulties of travel are the rough, bouldery substratum and the tangle of fallen logs that are everywhere in the way.

There is but little variation in this rich forest around the lake. It is modified, however, on drier sites and on the flood plain of the glacial stream west of the lake. . . .

Lunch. Raup family above Glacier Lake: Karl, David, Lucy, Hugh. Photo: Jim Soper.

[Brintnell Creek below the Lake]

East of the lake the stream that drains it soon enters a steep rapid which lies at the bottom of a picturesque winding gorge. The gorge is cut in shaly rocks whose dip is here nearly vertical. On the north side of the stream is a series of rocky and gravelly ridges separated by gently sloping plains covered with dry open woods. Occasional depressions are filled with muskegs. The open woods are composed of the following association:

PRIMARY SPECIES: white spruce var. *albertiana*, paper birch var. *commutata*, brown moss spp., grey and green reindeer lichen spp., other lichen spp.

This forest is rather park-like, with the trees standing in a dense mat of fruticose lichens and woodland mosses. . . .

[The Higher, South-Facing Forest]

The higher south-facing mountain slopes north of the lake, as well as gravel fans on that side, are notable for the addition of another variety of the white spruce, *Porsildii* . . . . The smooth, balsam-like bark of this species and its more broadly pyramidal form make it easily distinguishable in stands otherwise composed of var. *albertiana*. It was rarely seen on the south side of the lake.

As one ascends the steep mountain slopes north of the lake the forest gradually becomes more open, the trees smaller, and the ground cover composed of grasses and other herbs in place of the heavy moss mat of the lower slopes. At the same time the shrub layer changes in character. The substratum remains exceedingly rough and rocky, with its surface variously broken by gullies and ridges of glacial till. Most of the slope is blanketed with bouldery till which in places is arranged in ridges whose summits slope downward to the east. These appear to be lateral moraines deposited by the glacier which last filled the valley. Streams such as Frost Creek have cut gorges in the till, paving their beds with huge boulders that have been washed out of it. The channels of these streams evidently have shifted frequently, as shown by the abandoned gullies on either side.

The forests at 1000 - 1500 feet above the lake may be characterized as follows:

PRIMARY SPECIES: white spruce var. *albertiana, Porsildii*, common juniper var. *montana*, bear-berry or kinnikinnick, bunchgrass.

This forest is park-like, with the spruces branched from near the base. Where the substratum is fairly well-stabilized the openings among the trees are grassed over with the large tufts of altai fescue, interspersed with clumps of juniper and mats of kinnikinnick. Steeper slopes of gravel or loose shale, such as occur on the faces of the morainic ridges, lack most of the grasses and have only scattered juniper and kinnikinnick with a few herbaceous species that manage to gain a precarious foothold. It will be seen from the list of secondary species that this high slope forest combines elements of the floras of the rich lowland woods and the subalpine scrub.

Still higher on the mountainside, nearer timberline, the flora as a whole remains the same, but a somewhat different arrangement of primary species appears. Thickets of scrub birch, green alder, and gray-leaved willow var. *perstipula* begin to dominate the scene among the more scattered spruces, while on the loose soil of very steep slopes three-toothed saxifrage, lingenberry var. *minus*, and bog blueberry form low, patchy thickets among the juniper bushes.

[Burn Areas]

There is abundant evidence of fire on the mountainside in the neighborhood of Frost Creek. Evidence of at least two fires could be discerned, the later one probably less than 50 years ago. This later fire appears to have started near the western end of the lake and to have swept eastward and upward so as to consume all of the forest to timber line. Its eastern limit was not determined with accuracy, although from the appearance of the forest as seen from the lake it extended only a mile or so in that direction. In much older spruce forest near the shore about a mile east of Frost Creek some carbonized remains were found, indicating a much earlier fire. Other old forest in the vicinity gave no evidence of ever having been burned. It is difficult to see how these fires were started, unless they were ignited by lightning. Evidence of the presence of trappers or prospectors is all very recent, probably dating within the last 25 years, and nowhere around the lake is there any sign of Indian habitation. No old camp sites were found, and no trails other than occasional game trails.

[Slide Channels]

All of the great quantity of down timber, however, cannot be attributed to the fire, for there appears to be a normally high mortality rate among the trees on the steep slopes. This appears to be due both to land-slip and snow-slides, the latter probably by far more important. Views of the steep south-facing slopes from the mountains across the lake show what look like gullies, some of them extending all the way from timber line to lake level . . . .

They are not gullies in the ordinary sense, but great furrows in the forest, now in part overgrown with a dense tangle of willows and other shrubs of the bordering woods together with young spruce, aspen, and balsam poplar. At the foot of each furrow is an immense "jackstraw" tangle of dead logs. Neither the debris at the bottom of the slope or in the furrows themselves involves much mineral material, indicating that the damage has been done principally by sliding snow and ice.

At first glance the relative openness of the snow-slide furrows suggests that they would be good routes for climbing the mountain. Our party tried one but was very quickly disillusioned. The mass of debris on the ground and the matted tangle of downward-pointing branches on the distorted shrubs make climbing far more exhausting than it is in the neighboring forest.

The snowslide channels are seen only on very steep south-facing slopes. It is presumed that they are caused by the early loosening of snow during spring thaws at and above timber line. Insolation [flaking of rock when exposure to sun alternates with rapid cooling at night] would no doubt be more rapid here than under cover of forests at lower levels.

[Gravel Fans]

The great fans of gravel and stones that occur around the lake apparently are formed by torrential floods. The size of trees growing in the more active channels near the shore indicates that such floods are not frequent. None occurred during the season of 1939 that caused any noticeable displacement of materials. . . .

The surfaces of the fans are covered with gravel, stones, and boulders, the finer of which are nearest the lake. The general contours are of varying steepness depending upon the size of the materials. The slope of the one at the mouth of Frost Creek is rather gentle, about 200 feet in 1600; but some of those on the south shore, composed of large rocks from the steep north slopes of Colonel Mountain, have a much larger gradient, about 200 feet in 1000. The contours are broken by interlocking abandoned channels, some of which will no doubt become active again with the next flood.

The vegetation on the fans is an open forest of spruce, balsam poplar and large willows, interspersed with areas of nearly barren gravel or dense thickets of shrubs and young trees. The flatter parts which receive sufficient drainage, usually at the sides of the main channels, sometimes harbor muskegs. The drier parts proved to be of considerable floristic interest because of the heterogeneous mixture of species growing on them. Their flora is drawn not only from the woods and shores around the lake, but also from the alpine vegetation far above. . . .

PRIMARY SPECIES: white spruce var. *albertiana, Porsildii*, paper birch var. *humilis, commutata*, green alder, tea-leaved willow, felt-leaved willow var. *longistylis*, high-bush cranberry, soapberry, rose-hip.

[The Forest West of the Lake]

Still another type of white spruce forest has developed on the mud, sand and gravel flats west of Brintnell Lake. It is rather open and park-like with a mat of mosses that is thin and much interrupted . . . . This forest resembles flood plain types in other parts of the Mackenzie basin. It is of interest that marsh horsetail here forms dense green swards on the forest floor, much as meadow horsetail does along the Slave, Peace, and Athabaska Rivers.

[The Higher North-Facing Forests]

Most of the forests on the north-facing slopes fronting Brintnell Lake are radically different from those just described. White spruce timber similar to the more mesophytic type already noted occurs south of the lake, but is confined to the more stable portions of the alluvial fans, reaching only 200 feet above the shore. . . . The forests of the higher slopes are of black spruce.

The steep slopes are rocky, but they are covered for the most part by a thick mat of fruticose lichens and woodland mosses. This mat is often a foot or more in depth and is nearly always damp. It thins out gradually towards timber line, so that the underlying rocks begin to be exposed. The forest is an open one even at lake level, but it becomes still more so at higher elevations. The general aspect of the north-facing mountains is strikingly different from that of the opposite slopes, due to the peculiar greens of the fruticose lichens. These greens are particularly noticeable, of course, in wet weather, and contrast sharply with the higher grassy slopes north of the lake.

There is a certain amount of change in vegetation from bottom to top of the forested zone, but except for a narrow zone at the top the whole is sufficiently uniform to justify treating it as a unit. . . .

PRIMARY SPECIES: Trees: black spruce. Shrubs: grey-leaved willow var. *perstipula*, green alder, labrador tea, bog blueberry. Ground: reindeer lichen, cetraria lichen, brown mosses.

The primary species just noted are characteristic up to 500 - 600 feet above the lake. Above this general level Richardson's willow and scrub birch are added to those of the shrub layer, and smooth-leaved mountain-avens becomes an important component of the ground mat. The white birches disappear almost entirely from the association. Otherwise, the aspect is much the same except that the black spruces are more dwarfed and more widely spaced.

The upper 200 - 300 feet of the forest has a superficial resemblance to that below, but closer examination shows a striking change. The black spruce is replaced by white spruce var. *albertiana*, while the shrub and ground floras show a transition to the subalpine and alpine vegetation [with grey-leaved willow, var. *perstipula*, Richardson's willow, and scrub birch for shrubs, with reindeer and cetraria lichen and brown mosses on the ground. Soapberry is one of the secondary species].

This is the timber line community on the north-facing slopes. It gradually gives way to a subalpine scrub or to some form of alpine tundra, depending upon slope, exposure, or substratum. It is broken here and there by exposed cliffs of shale on which there is a ledge and crevice flora (see below), or by gullies in which the willows and alders make dense tangles of shrubbery.

We saw no evidence of fire in any part of the communities on the north-facing slopes.

[Muskegs]

Muskegs were observed on the low ground at both ends of Brintnell Lake, and on various local areas of small size on the mountain slopes and lake shores.

PRIMARY SPECIES: black spruce, tamarack var. *alaskana*, Labrador tea, sphagnum moss.

Pools and shores in the muskegs have a few floating or emergent aquatics . . . .

No raised bogs were seen, but on gentle, well-watered slopes the muskegs have a tendency, as in so many parts of the north, to spread upward.

Subalpine Scrub Communities

A shrub zone, or subalpine scrub, is not well defined on all the mountain slopes at Brintnell Lake. It is best seen on Red and Terrace Mountains north of the lake. Willows and dwarf birch make up most of it. On the steep north slopes of the glaciated facets of Colonel Mt. and on the hogbacks above them, it can scarcely be discerned at all. But on the flanks of the hogbacks there is usually a narrow band of shrubs which widens out somewhat in the intervening valleys. Here it occupies a strip probably less that 100 feet wide in vertical dimension.

The lip of the hanging valley from which Frost Creek falls into the main valley of the lake is about 3800 feet above sea-level, or about 1200 feet above the lake. The upper valley of Frost Creek is U-shaped below 5000 feet and evidently contained a tributary glacier at one time. Timber line on the south-facing slopes seems to be modified by the presence of the hanging valley. On Red and Terrace Mountains east and west of the Frost Creek valley it rises to nearly 5000 feet, but within the hanging valley itself there are only a few scattered and stunted trees above 4000 feet. Above timber on the south slopes there is only a narrow zone of scrub, which disappears completely on the steeper areas. This zone is greatly expanded in the hanging valley. It covers most of the valley bottom and the lateral slopes up to the tops of the morainic terraces, or to about 5000 feet. It thus achieves a vertical width of about 1000 feet.

Floristically the subalpine scrub is a transition, drawing most of its species from above and below . . . . A few species were found at Brintnell lake only in the subalpine scrub zone: Soper's sedge, red-stemmed saxifrage, epipsila violet, bunchberry (or dwarf dogwood), sweet coltsfoot, and arrow-leaved groundsel.

At timber line in the valley of Frost Creek the principal species are the willows, which form dense thickets 4-6 feet high. Along the stream itself felt-leaved willow becomes a primary species in place of grey-leaved willow. At higher elevations the shrubs of all kinds become dwarfed, and at the upper limits of the zone are often no more than a foot high. On the south and southeast slopes of Red Mountain the willows outnumber the dwarf birches; but on the east slope, as well as on the terraces of Terrace Mountain, dwarf birch forms nearly pure stands. Mountain heathers are much more prominent on the northeasterly slope of Red Mountain than elsewhere.

Throughout the scrub zone, but particularly toward its upper parts, the continuity of the thickets is much broken by grassy openings, in which altai fescue is a primary species. Most of the sedges and grasses as well as many of the other herbaceous plants . . . are found in these openings. A few, such as tall larkspur, mountain monkshood, and Jacob's ladder seem to find their most congenial habitat in the dense thickets. These thickets are difficult to climb through because their interlaced branches are depressed downward like those described in the snowslide areas.

Alpine Vegetation

It is nearly impossible to organize the alpine vegetation into clear-cut communities. . . . The nature of the alpine plant cover depends in large measure upon the stability of the soil and the amount of water at or near the surface. . . . Before beginning an account of the alpine vegetation some preliminary considerations are necessary. It will be noted that all our data on this type of habitat were gathered on the mountains of sedimentary rock. The granite peaks to the westward of Brintnell Lake were inaccessible in the time available, and probably are unscalable. Examined through field glasses they appeared to be nearly sterile, with the cliffs exfoliating so rapidly as to make plant life nearly impossible. The great talus at the foot of Mt. Harrison

Smith . . . is practically devoid of plants in many places, even nearly down to lake level.

A curious phenomenon of local distribution may also be pointed out there. A number of species were found to be absent or rare on one or the other of the mountains north and south of the lake. . . . Causes for these differences were not determined. They could be looked for in local climatic differences due to north and south exposure, or to variations in the chemical nature of the substratum. It is probable that there is more calcium in the rocks south of the lake than north of it, due to an abundance of calcite stringers in the shale. . . .

Damp Alpine Meadows

Damp alpine meadows at Brintnell Lake are best developed along small brooks where the latter flow over terraces of glacial till or other soil containing fines. They also appear on moderately sloping surfaces where snow lies in depressions well into the summer. Here the substratum may be of coarser debris because of the continued source of water from the melting snow. These snow-flush areas are commonly not so rich in species or individuals as brook valleys, for they are apt to become quite dry in late summer. Damp meadows make up, together, only a small part of the alpine vegetation, for surface water above timber line in these mountains is not common. They are usually formed in a thick turf which gives the impression of permanence and stability. It is common, however, to see large masses of this turf breaking up by transverse crevasses which produce an appearance of draped festoons when seen at a distance. They are thus constantly being dissected, later to form continuous mats again a little lower down the slopes.

PRIMARY SPECIES: felt and gray-leaved willow, Richardson's willow, Barratt's willow, scrub birch, graceful mountain sedge, altai fescue.

On many sites there is no small group of species that can be designated as primary, for the community is a hodge podge mixture of many.

Dry Alpine Meadows

Dry alpine meadows as I have conceived them here include a great variety of plant groupings. They occupy erosion and solifluction slopes that are fairly well stabilized but which have no continuous source of surface water except in the spring when most of the snow is melting. The mineral substratum is made of angular fragments of slate and shale, in some places comminuted to form a few inches of residual soil.

With the possible exception of slide rock, this type of vegetation covers more area than any other in the Brintnell Lake region. The long, even slopes of the gently rolling ancient surface seen from the air in the eastern parts of the Mackenzie Mountains are covered with it. It is represented at Brintnell lake on the summits of Red and Terrace Mountains, and probably on the upper south-facing slopes of Colonel Mt. It also appears on the lower parts of the great talus accumulations between 4000 and 6000 feet.

The primary group of species in the dry meadows varies greatly with exposure and the relative stability of the soil. . . . Variations . . . can best be shown by field notes made on primary species in various situations. The most complex aggregations are on slopes of northern and eastern exposure. Here a nearly continuous turf is sometimes formed, in which the PRIMARY SPECIES are smooth-leaved mountain-avens, four-angled mountain-heather, western fescue, net-veined willow, single-spiked sedge, bog blueberry var. *alpinum*, and mats of dwarfed scrub birch. Yellow mountain heather and crowberry are sometimes added to the list.

This complex was observed on the north slopes of Colonel Mountain, and on the north and east slopes of Red Mt.

The alpine surface of Red Mountain shows further variation as follows. At about 4800 feet on the south-facing slope is a rather open association of bog blueberry, altai fescue and a partial cover of lichens. Among the latter the xerophytic [dry-situated] coral lichen is predominant. Scrub birch are common in widely spaced, low mats. At about 5900 feet on the rounded slopes of the summit, the primary species are white mountain-avens, bog blueberry, and a lichen mat made up of *Cladonia* and *Cetraria*. Most of the ground is covered, but here and there are open areas of loose shale or finer soils kept barren by frost action. In depressions where snow had lain for a large part of the summer yellow mountain heather is abundant.

The highest point of Red Mt. is a narrow ridge on which a thin soil has weathered out of the shale. The most abundant plants are dwarfed Rocky Mountain fescue and a loose mat of *Cladonia* and *Cetraria*. In a few places there are mats of bog blueberry and four-angled mountain heather. The whole association is open, with much ledge and loose shale exposed.

Just east of the summit, at the beginning of a long slope of fairly well stabilized talus, the aspect changes at once. Here the primary species become altai fescue, four-angled mountain heather, white mountain avens, bog blueberry, and masses of fruticose lichens. At 5000 - 5500 feet on the easterly and northeasterly slopes this group is enlarged by the addition of crowberry and becomes the turf community described above.

Plants of Loose Slide Rock and Turf-Banked Terraces

Slide rock of loose, angular shale fragments is of wide occurrence above timber line . . . . In some places whole mountainsides are composed of continuous "rivers" of this shale. . . . The parent rock does not always break up into small pieces, however, so that here and there are masses of coarser material, forming steep slopes of large angular boulders. The shale is highly mobile, but the boulder fields are more or less stabilized and possess a flora similar to that of crevices and ledges. Only plants whose water requirements are low, and whose root and rhizome systems are adaptable in the extreme can live in loose shale. [Raup's list here includes many sedges, willows, mountain-avens, brabas, saxifrages, and *Arnicas* including *Arnica Snyderi*]

Except in certain instances . . . this assemblage of plants cannot be called a community in any sense. The shale is scarcely more than at an angle of rest, so that a touch is all that is needed to set it in motion. Most of the plants are widely scattered, and there are large areas completely devoid of vegetation of any kind. Roots and rhizomes are usually just beneath the surface, and nearly always extend up the slopes from the aerial parts of the plants. From a tiny, dwarfed herbaceous perennial, all alone in the loose and sliding shale and giving every appearance of being a chance seedling, one often can excavate an elaborate system of rhizomes and roots extending many feet up the slope and giving evidence of great age. Some plants of tufted habit seem to slide with the shale without serious damage.

The Vegetation of Stone Rings

Well-defined stone rings were observed at Brintnell lake . . . only on a deposit of glacial till in the upper valley of Frost Creek, at an altitude of about 4500 feet. The area where they were found is wet and springy, with small pools of water here and there. The rings vary in size from a few inches to about 6 feet, the larger ones bordered by till boulders as much as 3 feet in diameter.

The movement of materials by frost is so active that the stone rings are nearly devoid of vegetation except for crustose lichens on the larger boulders. A single species of vascular plant was growing sporadically in the stirred soil of the rings, red-stemmed saxifrage. Curiously enough, this species was found nowhere else in the region.

Ledge and Crevice Vegetation

Outcrops of creviced ledges occur on all the mountain slopes. Composed as they are largely of shaly rocks, they are breaking up very rapidly under the influence of subaerial erosion and frost cleavage. As stated previously, most of the sedimentary rocks of the region dip sharply to the southward and southwestward. Consequently the largest areas of shale slide-rock are on the south-and west-facing slopes, while the most extensive cliff development is on the upper north-facing ones. The north slope of Red Mountain, for instance, is a series of precipitous cliffs some 200 feet high, at the foot of which is a talus accumulation that reaches down another 300 feet or so to a small stream. Still higher cliffs appear on the north side of Colonel Mountain toward the summit. Hogback ridges are everywhere broken by steep outcrops of bedrock.

Most of the flora of the ledges is scattered in crevices or in small accumulations of residual soil that have formed on cliffs. . . . As on slide rock, it is nearly impossible to designate primary species. It might be proper to say that crustose lichens play this role, for they cover most of the bare rock. Among vascular plants, smooth-leaved mountain-avens, three-toothed saxifrage, sharp-tipped willow, and spike trisetum are probably the most common species. . . . It will be noted that this list has much in common with that for shale slide rock.

Plants of Ravines and Gorges below Timber Line

Rocky ravines and gorges near lake level have a flora drawn principally from the more dry-adapted elements of the slope forests. It is unnecessary to list it in full. Nevertheless these situations harbor a few unique species . . . . Two of the new species described in this paper, *Poa Brintnellii* (Brintnell's bluegrass) and *Lychnis brachycalyx*, were found in one of these [north slope of Colonel Mt.] gorges, as well as a species of saxifrage (*Saxifraga sibirica*) which proves to be an addition to the flora of the continent. These places are probably among the most difficult plant habitats which the region affords. They are subject to torrential floods, falling rock debris, rapid disintegration of the rock itself, and a growing season reduced to lowest terms. In many spots there is never any direct sunlight.

Ravines on the south-facing slopes are in sharp contrast. Their streams are lined with tall willows, and the forest flora pushes into every crevice and soil pocket. On the other hand, no plants of unusual geographic or taxonomic interest could be found in them.

Flood Plain Communities

A striking vegetational feature of the Brintnell Lake area is on the flood plain of the glacial stream at the western end of the lake. The youngest of the stream deposits are mud flats formed of the light gray rock flour brought down from the glacier. This material is in the form of a small delta at the mouth of the creek. A short distance above the lake coarser materials, sand and gravel, occur as low plains and ridges. Most of the sand and gravel appears to be coming from small tributary streams which come off the nearby mountainsides at steep gradients and spread their loads on the plain. Occasional torrential floods in the main creek probably are effective in reworking the sand and gravel.

I have already described the principal forest types on the flood plain, a white spruce type and a muskeg forest.

GEOGRAPHIC AFFINITIES OF THE VEGETATION OF SOUTH-WESTERN MACKENZIE

Introductory

Thus far I have attempted only to achieve botanical descriptions of some landscapes in southwestern Mackenzie. The geographic breadth of these descriptions and the amount of detail in them are extremely limited; but there are enough, I believe, to bring out the more important phytogeographic patterns in the area as a whole . . . .

Geographic Relationships of Species in the Brintnell Lake Area

Of the 283 species and varieties of vascular plants collected at Brintnell Lake, I have mapped 271 . . . . About 4.2% of the flora at Brintnell Lake (12 spp. and vars.) is composed of plants described as new . . . and I have not included any maps of them. They are as follows: *Picea glauca var. Porsildii, Poa Brintnellii, Carex Soperi, Salix Barrattiana* var. *marcescens, Salix Bebbiana* var. *depilis, Salix glauca* var. *perstipula, Lychnis brachycalyx, Saxifraga sibirica, Rosa acicularis* var. *cucurbiformis, Arnica alpine, Arnica Snyderi, Antennaria* sp.

[Raup now proceeds, using maps of Canada, to describe the "ranges" of plants found at Glacier Lake. He then describes the origin and dispersal of the plants - how they acquired their present ranges. Finally, he provides a]

CATALOGUE OF THE VASCULAR FLORA

[A list of 725 species and their descriptions and locations. Though Raup locates lichens and mosses, he does not catalogue them. Lucy Raup's collection of lichens is now being catalogued at Harvard's Farlow Herbarium. The following are Raup's descriptions and sketches of some new plants found around the lake, *Poa Brintnellii* (from pp. 112 - 114), *Carex Soperi* (129 - 131), and *Arnica Snyderi* (250 - 252)]

Poa Brintnellii

Open spruce woods on stony fan, south shore of Brintnell L. . ; mossy banks on an old shale slide in gorge, north slope of Colonel Mt., at. 3300' . . . . Common in the habitats noted; spikelets maturing about mid-August. Judging by its well-developed rhizomes this plant is in the section *Pratenses* and seems nearest to *P. arctica*, which has a spreading inflorescence with spikelets only at or near the tips of the branches. However, its glabrous internerves, rather prominent intermediate nerves (especially in mature specimens), and its tall sprangling habit distinguish it from *P. arctica*. Also the bases of spikelets are not so much rounded . . . . In spikelet characters it somewhat resembles *P. paucispicula* or *P. leptocoma*, but neither of these pro-

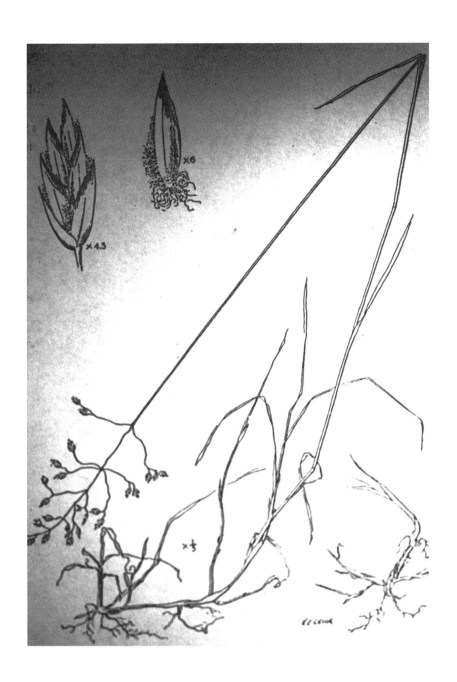

Poa brintnelli

107

×½

× 7.5

Carex Soperi

108

duces such prominent rhizomes. Its inflorescence also resembles that of *P. nervosa*, but the latter has no cobweb at the base of the lemma . . . .

Carex Soperi

Damp grassy place in willow-birch scrub, upper valley of Frost Cr., north of Brintnell L., alt. 4000'. Common in this situation but not seen elsewhere. In flower characteristics and the general appearance of leaves and culms these plants closely resemble *C. festivella Mackenzie*, but they differ from this as well as from most of the section *Ovales* in being non caespitose. The culms rise singly or few together at intervals of several inches, and must be collected individually like those of *C. siccata*.

Arnica Snyderi

Alpine crevices and rock slides, north slope of Colonel Mt., July 5; shale cliffs in gorge on north slope of Colonel Mt., alt. 3500'; loose slide rock on south slope of Red Mt., alt. 5500' - 5900'; high shale slopes on west side of Terrace Mt., alt. 5500' - 6000'.

Common in the Brintnell L. area; found flowering in July and early August. This beautiful species has the single nodding heads and semi-scapose habit of the far northwestern group which contains *A obtusifolia* and *A. Lessingii*. It is separated from these, however, by its yellowish brown anthers and white pappus. In these characters it resembles *A. Louiseana* Farr, which has proved to be of wide range in boreal America . . . . When compared with an isotype of *A. Louiseana* at the Gray Herbarium, our plants prove to be much more scapose, with the leaves nearly or quite entire, whereas they are saliently dentate in *A. Louiseana*. In the latter the leaves are glandular puberulent on both sides, and ovate- or obovate-lanceolate, while in *A. Snyderi* they are glabrous beneath, glabrous or sparingly glan-

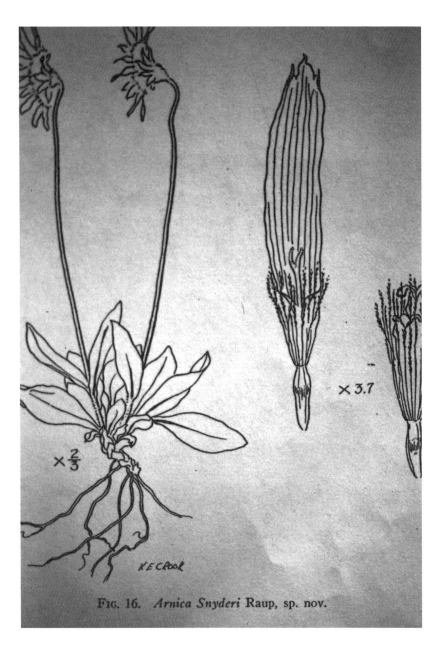

$\times \frac{2}{3}$

$\times 3.7$

K E CROOK

FIG. 16. *Arnica Snyderi* Raup, sp. nov.

dular-papillose above, and are commonly broadly ovate to rhombic-ovate. In leaf shape they resemble some small forms of the eastern representative of A. Louiseana originally described by Fernald as A. Griscomi . . . but the latter, now reduced to a subspecies of A. Louiseana, has the character-

110

istically denticulare leaves. Furthermore, our plants have the upper parts of the stem and the base of the involucre yellowish brown-lanate, while in *A. Louiseana ssp Griscomi* they are merely villous or villous-hirsute with white hairs. . . . *A. Louiseana* belongs in the group which centers around *A. alpina*, and its heads are not truly nodding but bent over in drying or wilting. All of our field notes, however, state that the peduncles of *A. Snyderi* were bent while the flowers were in anthesis, straightening later. It is true, however, that the bend is not a sharp one as in *A. Lessingii*, and it may be that our plants' affinities are with the *A. alpina* group.

Raup camp at the west end of Glacier Lake, 1939. The
water bags hanging on the trees were kept filled by Karl
and David Raup

Excerpts from <u>The Camper's Cookbook</u> by Lucy G. Raup. Tuttle, 1967.

Sometimes camp cookbooks are put together by reassembling gleanings from other cookbooks. They are compilations. Others have their beginnings in basic home cooking tried out in camp and the results appraised. . . . This little book has evolved by the second method.

Voluminous notes were kept on twenty-odd camping trips ranging in length from over-night to two-and three-month journeys in the Canadian North. The means of travel covered the gamut of possibilities, from walking with a pack to modern air transport. The number of people to be planned for . . . varied from two to fourteen. . . . Changes in recipes and the new ones developed were recorded at the time, commonly with menus and the supplies used in them. At the end of each trip an inventory was made and used to revise the gear and grub lists for the next trip.

Notes of this kind are useful as data from which to make a camp cookbook. But anyone who cooks knows that they are lifeless without the addition of person skills and something that has to be called "flair." Only this can transform the raw data into a genuine campers' cookbook. The author of this book has always liked to cook . . . .

CHOCOLATE PIE
2 tsp. Crisco
6 tbsp. flour
1 1/2 cup milk
1 sq. unsweetened chocolate
3/4 cup sugar
1/4 tsp. salt
2 egg yolks (if available)
1 tsp. vanilla
2 tbsp. granulated sugar (if available)
2 egg whites (if available)
Baked pie shell

Melt Crisco. Add chocolate and keep over low fire until chocolate is melted (stirring constantly). Add flour, sugar, salt, milk. Bring slowly to boil, stirring constantly until thick and smooth. Remove from fire and add egg yolk. If eggs are available, make a meringue by whipping 2 whites until stiff, add 2 tbsp. sugar. Place meringue on top of pie and brown in moderate heat.

BREAD PUDDING
4 cups old bread
4 cups milk
2 eggs or equivalent
1 tbsp. butter
1/2 cup sugar
Vanilla (if available)
Salt

Heat milk and add butter, sugar, and bread broken into small pieces. Let stand 20 minutes, then add eggs (beaten if fresh) vanilla and salt. Pour into a greased pan and place the pan in a larger pan of hot water. Bake about one hour or until the pudding does not adhere to a knife blade inserted to the centre of the pudding. Serve hot with hard sauce or cold with milk or other sauces.

Fruit Bread Pudding. Add 1/3 cup cooked fruit, jam, marmalade, or raisins to the pudding before baking. The sugar may need to be increased for some fruits.

Chocolate Bread Pudding. To the basic recipe add 1 ounce of baking chocolate or 1/4 cup of cocoa (mixed with the sugar). Increase the sugar in the original recipe to 1 cup. This is a real party dessert if served hot with hard sauce.

HARD SAUCE
1/4 cup butter
3/4 cup sugar
1 tbsp. hot water (rum or brandy is better)
Vanilla (omit if rum or brandy is used)

Cream butter, add sugar slowly. Add vanilla and hot water a few drops at a time, continuing to cream the mixture. When the mixture is well creamed, serve on a hot pudding.

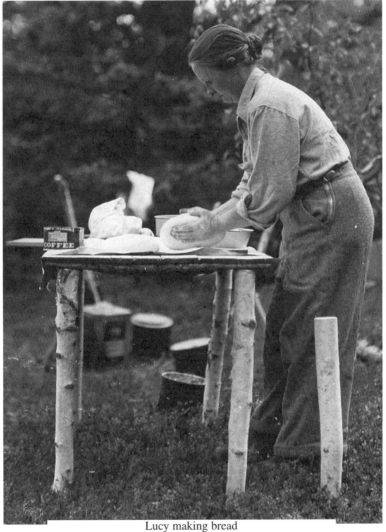
Lucy making bread

Lucy cooking. Note the forked stick used to keep the pot close to the fire.

HOT WATER PIE CRUST
1 cup shortening (slightly softened)
3 cups flour (approximately)
1/2 cup boiling water
1/2 tsp. baking power (optional)
Salt

Place shortening in a bowl or pan and pour the boiling water over it. Add salt, then flour and baking powder until no more can be stirred in. Divide the dough in two pieces, one for upper and one for lower crust. Roll dough into thin sheets. This amount of dough makes a double crusted pie for a reflector pan 18 by 7 inches.

FRUIT PIE

Line a pie pan with a crust made by the above recipe. Sprinkle it with 4 tbsp flour and 2 tbsp sugar. Pour into this the fruit, enough to fill a pan (a reflector pan 18 by 7 inches takes 1 1/2 to 2 lbs of dried apricots or peaches). If dried fruit is used, it must be previously cooked; fresh fruit need not be. Sprinkle a little flour (about 2 tbsp) and a little sugar (about 2 tbsp) over the fruit. Moisten the upper edges of the lower crust. Place over it the upper crust, which has had a few small holes made in it either in the form of a design or just holes. Press the two edges together tightly, trim off any extra dough. Crimp the edges between thumb and fingers so that the juice may not escape. Bake in moderately hot heat at 450 degrees for 15 minutes and then at 350 degrees for 30 to 40 minutes.

[Note: Lucy Raup favored the use of the reflector oven]: Excellent and much lighter in weight than a Dutch oven. It can produce equally good baked food. Its operation is more easily mastered because the food in it is visible at all times. It does require more fuel than the Dutch oven. The reflector oven is nothing more than two slanting pieces of aluminum or tin which reflect the heat from a fire in front of them upon a pan midway between them. The ends are closed and all pieces are hinged together so that when not in use the reflector may be folded. . . . The baking pan is best made of dark steel, because it absorbs rather than relects heat. When the pan is new there may be some difficulty in keeping it from rusting. A light greasing with a bacon rind is effective. To secure best results with a reflector, it must be bright and shiny, so it is well to carry a small cake of bon-ami or mild scouring powder. Lava soap does very well, is compact and easily carried.

James H. Soper and Hugh Miller Raup. Journal Entries about the Arnold Arboretum Expedition to Glacier Lake, 1939.

(For easy cross-referencing, We've placed Raup's Journal side-by-side with Soper's, <u>Raup's in plain text and Soper's in italics</u>. Soper's journal, which he accurately refers to as his Diary since it records the events of every day, begins with a photo of him sitting on a log raft moored at the delta at the west end of the lake. He is sitting on a wooden box, his legs crossed, writing or sketching. The Diary ends with a photo of the MAS float plane that took them in and out, the Cathedral in the background. The Diary begins with a Note: "The expedition comprised Dr. Hugh M. Raup [botanist, Harvard Univ.], his wife, Lucy Raup [lichenologist], their two sons: Karl Raup [age 9], David Raup [age 6], and James H. Soper [age 23], field assistant [recent graduate student from McMaster Univ., B.A. 1938, M.A. 1939]."

The Diary was mailed to us by Soper when we contacted him through the Canadian Museum.

We transcribed Raup's Journal from his leather-bound notebook entitled "Record: Journals 1939" and, on inside page, "Journal — Summer 1939." The notebook is located at the University of Alberta Book and Record Depository or BARD, Acc. No: 97-113, Box 2.)

<u>JOURNALS</u>

20 May - Lucy and the boys left Boston about 1:00 p.m. for Springfield and Minneapolis. I finished packing and straightening up the house and left at 8:45 for Ottawa.

21 May - Porsild met me at Bank St. Station. Saw King and Queen and Government House.

22 May - [meets Soper and talks about Soper's work next year at Harvard; arranges for a radio licence in Soper's name as a Canadian licencee; lunches with Jenness and Porsild] Had a long and very profitable talk with Jenness who, I think, is one of the men who will do most for the National Museum.

25 May - *Boarded the train at 9:55 p.m. in Hamilton and felt very lonely as I looked through the window while waiting for the train to leave. Changed trains and went to bed immediately upon arriving in Toronto (11:00 p.m.).*

26 May - *Passing through northern Ontario. The trees are just turning green in this district (Fayelot). Great extents of swamp and muskeg with black spruce, leatherleaf, etc. Evidences of glaciation in the sand and till, also much granite rock and burned-over areas with new poplar stands. Had dinner with a chap from Ottawa (in Medicine at Queens) on his way to be a caddy at Jasper Park Lodge.*

27 May - *Had breakfast in the Winnipeg station restaurant . . . . The day riding across the prairies seemed very long and tiresome. Finally arrived in Saskatoon.*

28 May - [Edmonton] Lucy, Karl and Dave arrived early in a.m. and we got established in the MacDonald Hotel.

29 May - Soper arrived. // *Arrived in Edmonton at 6:30 p.m. and was met by Dr. Raup. Breakfasted with all Raup family in the Macdonald Hotel cafeteria. Went shopping in morning and afternoon and bought shirts, pants, socks and shoes. . . . Had supper with R.G. Cormack at the home of Dr. & Mrs. E. H. Moss and visited the University and Botany Departments. Saw grandstands for Royal Visit along Portage Ave. Spent the night with Dr. & Mrs. Moss.*

30 May - *Returned to the hotel, got haircut and called at the post office for mail. Left Edmonton with the Raups at 11:00*

*a.m. by train for Waterways. Arrived at Lac la Biche at 7:15
p.m. and saw first new plants.*

31 May - *We arrived at Waterways at 6:30 a.m. and checked
in at the Waterways Hotel. Walked to MacMurray in the
afternoon and collected willows. Wrote four letters and five
cards.*

1 June - *Posted letters and collected plants along bank of
Clearwater River.*

2 June - *We climbed the hill behind the hotel and collected
plants. Got on board the "Pelly Lake" at 10:00 p.m. in readi-
ness for an early sailing next morning. A small diesel-pow-
ered tug-boat pushing one large and two small barges in front
of it. Other passengers included two geological survey par-
ties.*

3 June - Boarded "Pelly Lake" 11 p.m., left Waterways about
4 a.m. // *The boat started down the river at dawn and was
soon in the Athabaska River.*

4 June - *Still proceeding down the Athabaska but soon got
into the delta floodplain region. Reached the mouth about
5:00 p.m. and left barges by river edge while proceeding to
aid of the "Athabaska River" which was stuck on a sandbar in
the lake near the river mouth. Towed one of its barges back to
river mouth by which time the stern-wheeler had gotten free of
the bar. Crossed the lake at dusk and reached Chipewyan
about midnight, leaving early the next morning.*

5 June - *Started down the Slave River channel which was
against the current at this time of year. Soon reached place
where the Peace River enters the Slave and then proceeded
with the current in our favour. Stopped with food for wood
cutters and put a trapper ashore. Reached Fitzgerald about
6:30 p.m. and took a taxi across the 16-mile portage to Fort*

Smith. Arrived at the Mackenzie Hotel, of the Hudson Bay Co . . . . Still accompanied by the two geological parties of Drs. Lord and Joliffe.

6 June - *Spent the day making arrangements re transportation and re-packing.*

7 June - *Made final arrangements re flying out of Smith as did Drs. Joliffe, Lord and their parties. Met our pilot Archie Vanhee, who is to take us to Simpson tomorrow.*

8 June - Left Smith on plane (MAS) with pilot Archie Van Hee . . . . Had a grand trip to Simpson, 400+ miles . . . . Vast areas of prairie south of Great Slave Lake and on both sides of upper Mackenzie . . . Beautiful colors in sloughs — orange-red to bright green. Must be algal. Most of west arm of lake full of ice, blown there by S.E. Wind (?). Put up camp at Simpson in RCM Police lot. Good camp site. Got our tents and grub after having a lunch at Whitcombs. Tents and camping gear in N.T. Warehouse, grub at H. B. Co — All in good shape. Got supper in Police house — fine hospitality. // *Tried to take off but due to weather conditions were unsuccessful in the first attempt and had to leave behind Mr. Lawrence and baggage in order to reduce weight. The second attempt was successful and had the thrilling experience of rising over the Smith rapids and circling the Fort to gain altitude before heading north. The plane rode quite smoothly and no one was sick, although none of us had flown before. Got a marvellous idea of the country and was impressed by the great extent of the prairies, sloughs, rivers and forests. Saw quantities of ice while crossing Great Slave Lake and arrived at Fort Simpson 3 hrs and 5 mins. later. Had lunch at Andy Whittington's store and then set up camp in the RCMP lot, having our supper at their house.*

9 June - Talked to Father Vachet (sp?) — 70 years old. He came here in 1895 . . . . // Set up our own camping system and met the Anglican parson, Harry Cooke, and his wife. A plane came in tonight but was unable to land on account of bad weather and a rough river.

10 June - 16 June - We made acquaintance with a number of people . . . . Dr. Truesdale is government medical officer and Indian Agent. We spent a delightful evening at his home where we met his wife. They have a sizeable farm with cows and chickens. Their gardens are well up. Hothouses are used to start some things. They have one son just about Karl's age. Mr. and Mrs. Isbister entertained us one evening. He is in charge of the government radio station . . . . There are 3 other men at the station, all married. Mr. and Mrs. Cook proved among the most interesting folk we met. We were in their house frequently. Mr. Cook is pastor of the Anglican mission, and together they run the Anglican Mission school. They have one son about two years old. They are well read and exceed-ingly intelligent. They should go places. Not ordinary mis-sionaries! Mr. and Mrs. James Cree . . . manager Northern Traders Co . . . recently sold out to HBC, [so] he has bought out the local property and is going to trade independently. Andy Whittington runs a sort of combination hotel, restaurant and trading post. He is the town character — a great talker and "anti" almost everything. Lucy went through the hospital and met the grey nuns who serve as nurses. // *10 June - The bad weather developed into an all-day rain and we were forced to stay around camp. Visited the RCMP boys [Stuart and Littlewood] in the evening, meeting George Souter, and enjoying the warm cabin and refreshments. 11 June - We went collecting and followed trails to the other side of the island and back again. 12 June - Spent the day around camp and in the evening went to the radio station and visited with the Isbisters. Developed a head cold! 13 - 14 June - Confined to camp by my head cold and stomach disorder. Took Vick's cure and lime-juice diet. 15 June - Back to normal eating today. The mail plane arrived in the evening and I received three let-ters. The plane proceeded to Norman.*

16 June - We were landed at the western end of Brintnell Lake shortly after 8 p.m. The canyons of the South Nahanni are breath-taking, but no more so than the jagged snow-capped mountains of the Snyder Range which lies west of Brintnell Lake. We have never seen such rough mountains. Randall had never flown this course before, but he found our destination without difficulty . . . he had to do his circling out in the broader valley of the S. Nahanni and then come in to the lake low enough to land without circling. . . . We set up camp hurriedly and got a fair night's sleep. We camped on the same site used by the Snyder party two years ago. We found plenty of tent poles and stakes, a cooking and eating table rigged for a shelter, a disintegrating raft, and an old sectional canoe with the bottom knocked out of it. *// The plane returned and we packed everything and took off in the Mackenzie Air Service's big "Ballanca" for Brintnell Lake. The plane rode very smoothly and we passed over much flat country before reaching the Nahanni River region. Crossed two or three picturesque mountain ranges of undescribable beauty and took pictures from the cabin windows. Finally flew past Virginia Falls and recognized Brintnell Lake by the shape seen on the map. Had to circle within the parallel mountain ranges before we were low enough to enter the valley and make a sweeping landing on Brintnell Lake at the Snyder campsite below Cathedral. Unloaded and said farewell to the plane. Had supper and put up our tents.*

17 June - *Spent the day setting up camp: made a ladder, fireplace, eating-shelter and food-cache.*

18 June - *Further work on the campsite. Made plant-press dryer. Had baked beans for supper.*

19 June - [Both Soper and Raup start recording min. and max. temperatures in Fahr., indicated here in bold print] **42/69** *Started collecting plants today. Had bran muffins for supper.*

20 June - **42/69** *Collected along the lakeshore. "Pops' [Dr. Raup] caught two fish which we fried for supper. Also had lemon pie.*

21 June - **45/69** *Climbed the mountain back of camp and west of the stream. Collected en route. Others started to descend in order to reach camp in time for radio broadcast schedule but I pushed on to the summit (2500 - 3000') and had wonderful view of the next range and intervening shaley valleys. Bluish snow pile on top. Took pictures. Rejoined the others and finally reached camp all tired out and with sore feet. Hot soup tasted very good and retired to a comfortable bed.*

22 June - **45/67** *Had quite a rainstorm today so spent the day pressing the plants from yesterday's collections.*

23 June - **41/67** Jim and I went west along the lake shore to the end of the lake, then tried to follow a trail still further westward along the base of the slope to a big rock slide that we can see from camp. This trail proved so tangled with downed timber, however, that we had to give up the idea of making the trip in the limited time available. // *Spent the morning collecting from the SW end of the lake — in marshy ground, muskeg, along shore by the iron spring. Spent the afternoon pressing plants.*

24 June - **39.5/75.5** Jim and I and the boys fixed up the raft so we can use it. This raft was left by the Snyder party along with the sectional canoe. The latter has a great hole clear through the bottom of the middle section . . . . Two canoe paddles were left with the sectional canoe. The raft worked alright, but proved too unwieldly for extensive navigation. We collected a few things from the mud flats at the mouth of the creek. // *Went out for wood and dried our plant specimens today.*

25 June - **45/67** *Did a washing today and dried plants. Built a stone fireplace.*

26 June - **41/69** *Pops and I climbed the mountain back of camp and west of the stream by following the trail up the creek canyon and further up the glacial valley above. Collected and took pictures.*

27 June - **48/63** The insufficiency of the raft for our needs forces us to see what we can do with the battered canoe. It looks as though some animal, a moose or a bear, had simply tramped the middle section to pieces . . . . By putting some stout dry spruce poles lengthwise in the bottom of the middle section we got a framework on which to piece together the bits of rib and planking that made up the bottom. *// Pressed plants and worked on the canoe. Had bran muffins and lemon pie for supper.*

28 June - **51/61** *Muggy weather today. Pressed plants and worked on the canoe. NOTE: The canoe was a three-part sectional canoe with bow and stern fastened to centre section with butterfly bolts. It had been upturned on the ground during the winter and something [probably a bear] had stepped on the centre section and made a large hole. We covered the hole with a sheet of tin from a large bacon container, then put canvas over the tin and sealed the cracks with spruce gum.*

29 June - **47/69** Lucy and the boys spent a considerable part of the day gathering spruce gum which we melted up and used to seal joints and seams . . . . It leaked very little and was distinctively serviceable. *// Gummed the canoe and Mrs. Raup [Lucy] and I tried it out again after supper by trolling in the lake. Lucy sighted a moose on the other side of the lake and we got close enough for a good view. Returned to camp for Pops and his rifle and then started across for the other side of the lake. The moose was standing on the shore watching us and so we approached fairly close. Pops took a shot at him.*

The moose jumped into the water and splashed away for a few minutes while we kept a respectful distance. Finally he stopped kicking and we approached and dragged the body up onto the gravelly beach. Pops built a fire while Lucy and I returned for knives and utensils and by firelight we cut off his hind and forequarters and skinned them. Returned to camp with this large quantity of fresh meat, which we stored up on the food cache still with the smell of warm blood on our hands.

30 June - **47/69** *Pops and I towed the moose carcass down the lake to get it away from our camp. Had moose steaks for dinner and roasted moose for supper. Collected and pressed plants.*

1 July - **48/68** Found Snyder's pole table and utilized it. *// It rained nearly all day; so we worked around camp and cooked up some moose meat.*

2 July — **45/67** *Lucy and I cooked up and "canned" moose meat and broth for soup stock. I had a bath and a "plunge" in the lake. Water temperature was 56 F [!!] and the air 63.*

3 July — **47/68** This day we all went in the canoe to the east end of the lake. Left after breakfast and got back about mid-afternoon. We followed the north shore east to a "narrows," stopping to collect in a muskegy place. Found a well-built cache and a burned cabin at the east end, at the head of the small stream which drains the lake, and stopped there for a little collecting . . . . Followed the south shore most of the way back to camp.

4 July — **42/68** *Collected and pressed plants and brought in firewood. After supper had some fireworks to celebrate the date.*

5 July — 39/73 We all spent the day on Colonel Mtn opposite camp. Left the canoe at the mouth of the creek which enters the lake from the west, and started up the Mtn about 10:30. It was about 3:00 when we finally got above timber and found a small, snow-fed creek where we could eat our lunch. // *We all climbed Colonel Mt. to about the 2500' level and collected many new numbers.*

6 July — 44/72 *Spent the day pressing plants from previous days.*

7 July — 42/72 *Pressed plants and wrote up field notes.*

8 July — 42/74 Moose steaks improving as the meat hangs over the lake in the shade [sketch of the rig, which includes netting to keep off bugs] // *Did a washing and took a "swim" in the lake.*

9 July — 46/67 [Raup mentions that they couldn't get Snyder's canoe up Brintnell Creek; the creek is too shallow. Also mentions that the radio doesn't work well, has put them in contact with Fort Simpson only a couple of times, though they can generally *hear* Simpson] // *Wrote notes and investigated a stream into the river flats. Grilled bacon for breakfast.*

10 July — 44/64 *Collected in the lowlands delta region and gravelly ridges at west end of the lake. Went a good distance towards the talus slope of Cathedral. Collected* Sphlachnum *moss for the first time. Returned to camp and just got lunch cooked before a heavy rainstorm set in, which lasted all day. Pressed our plants. Heard Simpson by radio but could not answer as the radio went out of commission.*

11 July — 46/50 *It rained all day so we pressed plants. Started a soap carving of a marten.*

12 July — **45/63.5** *Brought in wood and dried plants. Lost our supply of canned moose meat due to blowflies. Radio was repaired today and got a message through to Simpson for the first time.*

13 July — **47/60** *Emptied our presses and sawed wood. Chopped firewood and pressed a few grasses. Went trolling after supper without success and had to return on account of rain. The weather has been unsettled for the last few days with frequent showers.*

14 July — **39/68** Clear and beautiful day! We all set out about 9:30 A.M. in another attempt to reach the big rock slide at the base of Cathedral Mtn. We went by way of the flat land in the valley as far as we thought we could, then took to the mountain side north of the valley. On the way out we kept at an elevation of perhaps 200' above the creek, and soon found that Cathedral Mtn is made of granite rather than limestone as we thought. Most of the slide rock, stabilized and otherwise, that we crossed was of this light gray granite. We crossed the contact about half-way between camp and the base of Cathedral . . . The going was difficult and dangerous along this steep, rock-strewn slope. Most of it is heavily forested and moss-covered, so that one is continually stepping into rocky holes. We finally reached the edge of the slide about 4 p.m., and were finally kept from examining it closely by a rocky torrent which descends into the valley just at the eastern base of the big mountain . . . . The slide itself is evidently quite sterile except at the very base where a few trees and bushes grow. It is *active* and the almost vertical faces of the mountain are rapidly exfoliating. We could see many freshly exposed surfaces, and here at camp we frequently hear fragments thundering down the slides to the talus.

15 July — **40/68** Mosquitos have been very bad for the past week. We have a continual smudge going in camp when getting meals and eating. // *[Soper records max as **74**] Pressed*

128

the plants of yesterday's collection. Collected a few more around camp. Put the fish net out. Had a squash pie today.

16 July — **45.5/74** *Collected at the west end of the lake. Dried plants and took flower pictures.*

17 July — **51/68** Dried plants and drew fungi. Had chocolate bread pudding for supper. Continues to be cloudy and overcast.

18 July — **44/75** *Up at 5 A.M. to get breakfast and start early on mountain climbing. Went up the mountain behind camp and west of the creek to the upper valley and then crossed to the east side of the stream and climbed the slope to a point 3020' above the lake [2640']. Had marvellous collecting in the high stream valley.*

19 July — **45/78** *Spent the day pressing our plants from yesterday.*

20 July — **49/78.5** *Wrote field notes and started plants drying. Took a bath and swim in the lake.*

21 July — **53.5/83.5** *Chopped wood and took a swim in the morning. Changed to summer clothes. Got [i.e. cooked or prepared] the three meals today. Dry plants removed from the press.*

22 July — **60/71** *Cook for the day. Drew fungi and read.*

23 July — **48/69** *Muggy, unsettled. Had good contact with Simpson in the evening and could hear their phone clearly for the first time. // Started on a trip to the end of the lake but threatening weather caused us to return to camp. Collected a few plants around camp before rain. Heard Simpson's message by voice tonight.*

24 July — 47/63 We left the canoe at the site of the burnt cabin just below where the stream leaves the lake, and walked eastward, partly on trails over muskegs and rocky or sandy ridges, to where the stream from the lake passes through a rocky, shaly gorge. . . . After lunch we went north from the cabin site, up a slope timbered with birch and white spruce, with black spruce in the muskegs. A blazed trail we followed soon petered out . . . . It took us about an hour and a half to paddle home, approx 3 miles. BOTANICAL NOTES: East of the lake the stream which drains it soon enters a steep rapid which lies in the bottom of a picturesque winding gorge in shaly rocks. The dip of these rocks here is nearly vertical, and the shale flakes off very easily and very rapidly. There is a series of rocky knolls along the stream (north side) separated by gently sloping plains containing open woods or muskegs. The open woods are white spruce and birch standing in a dense mat of bunch lichens and woodland mosses.// *Made a canoe trip to east end of the lake and collected all along the river as far as the rapids. Saw* Pinguicula.

25 July — 44/65 *Pressed plants and got wood today.*

26 July — 44/70 Jim has turned out to be quite capable and willing as a cook. This gives Lucy considerably more time for sorting and cleaning lichens than she has had before. This is the first time she is taking home a cleaned and numbered col-lection. // *Dried plants and sawed wood. Got supper with scalloped potatoes and ham. Had a haircut.*

27 July — 42/67 *Got up early to start on mountain climbing trip but stayed in camp on account of threatening weather. Did some plankton towing and worked around camp. Finished drying plants and removed them from the presses.*

28 July — 37.5/58.5 The top of the slope up [Colonel Mtn] from the lake ends in a point, which is the beginning of a long, sharply defined hog-back that extends to the summit of the mountain. The sides fall away sharply, often from a ridge just wide enough to walk on . . . . The hogback itself is broken in several places by sharp cliffs and local summmits. We followed the top of the hogback up to 6000', detouring around the steep cliffs and clambering up the siderock on their flanks. Had lunch on a local summit at about 4800'. BOTANICAL NOTES: On the map Lambart makes the first 4-500' above the lake somewhat less steep than the slope further up. Our observations scarcely show this.

29 July — 46/68 *Spent the day putting in the press the plants from yesterday. The squirrels are now tame enough to let you pet them if there is a strong attraction like fresh bread. Stayed up to cook the prunes for breakfast.*

30 July — 46/58 This morning a small flock of gulls appeared on the lake. We have had 2 or 3 greyish or dun-colored gulls all summer, but these have white heads and bodies, and the wings have black tips. They have yellowish color on the undersides of their bodies . . . . Heard a sand-hill crane today, the second time within a week or two . . . . There is a well-worn game trail all along the south shore of the lake, with many moose tracks on it . . . . Our porcupine continues to frequent camp. He is an immense one, with yellow quills. He must be 3' long overall. We discourage him on all occasions, and drive him away. He must be terribly dumb and slow-witted . . . . The squirrels are getting more tame all the time . . . . They will eat from our hands and the other day Jim managed to stroke one. // *Wrote field notes for Friday's collections and drew fungi. Chopped wood.*

31 July — 39/62 *Climbed spruce trees for cones. Did a washing.*

1 Aug — 42/61 *Removed some plants from press but most of the fleshy things were not dry.*

2 Aug — 41/60 Jim, Karl and I took some lunch and started out on the trail that leads NE from camp along the wooded mountain slope. The trail is blazed, but otherwise very poorly marked. We followed it about a mile and then lost it. It takes a nearly straight course through the woods, gradually rising to about 450' above the lake. [They go up over a series of shoulders to about 5000'] Found a trail, well worn, running E-W. On it we found a lob-sticked tree. . . . Had a good radio contact with Simpson in the evening. Heard their phone conversation fairly well. They report that Mr. Harry Snyder is in the country by plane, and will be in our district about Aug. 14. There are 7 men in the party. Isbister thought they were mostly mining and oil men. He didn't know how long they would be here. // *Karl, Pops and I walked along hills back of camp and back to the mountain slopes above the creek gorge. Got a few plants and mushrooms. Saw two moose on the hillside. Heard that a party of Snyder's men are to come into this district for a few days in about two weeks.*

3 Aug — 42/64 The water in the lake has lowered about a foot in the past week or two, making a lot of wet meadow land about the mouth of the glacier stream passable on foot. // *Put plants in press and collected along opposite shore of lake and stream.*

4 Aug —40/57 Cold, damp morning, with cold rain and mild squalls down the valley all day, alternating with a few bits of bright sunshine. There was new snow on the mountains for the first time, some on the north slope of Colonel Mtn down as low as 4500 or 5000'.

5 Aug — 40/56 Tried fishing with no success. // *Got in wood and drew fungi.*

6 Aug — 32/59.5 Picked enough blueberries for a pie, at the iron spring. // *Collected at end of lake and picked enough berries for a pie.*

7 Aug — 38/70 *Climbed the mountain behind camp and reached the summit. Returned by north-east slope.*

8 Aug — 43/72 *Pressed plants from yesterday. Had chocolat pie for supper dessert.*

9 Aug — 40/75.5 *Labelled plants, dried plants, drew fungi, dried fungi, sawed wood. Took a bath and plunge in the lake.*

10 Aug — 44/72 We are having another warm spell and the lake has risen again, about a foot. Its level appears to depend on heat rather than rainfall, at least at this season, for it is fed largely by melt water from the glaciers up the valley. // *Sketched Cathedral.*

11 Aug — 51/64 *Took plants out of presses and cleaned up the campsite.*

12 Aug — 46/64 *Went blueberry picking in the morning and got enough for 3 pies. The porcupines have been eating the top off our table. Start of another rainy spell began just after supper.*

13 Aug — 43/51 *Rained most of the day so worked around camp.*

14 Aug — 36/40 The Snyder party left Simpson at 7:30 and were here by 9:45 without difficulty. There were 9 men — Snyder and 3 of his business friends who were hunting in this region, pilot Bob Randall and two mechanics (they came in the same plane that brought us), the packer Jim Ross, and a cook. They had been hunting at Sheep lake, N of here, and had come to Simpson via Norman. They were headed for Tuchodi Lake for more hunting. They set up a camp and shared their mess with us. In the late afternoon, most of them tried hunting or fishing along the lake, all without success. //

Radioed the weather at 6:30 a.m. and Snyder party arrived at 9:45 a.m.

15 Aug — 40/58 The Snyder party left about mid-morning . . . . I had a long talk with Mr. Snyder in the morning about the affairs of the National Museum and Herbarium, and about plans for the "boreal Flora." We have made tentative arrangements to visit him in Montreal late in October or early in November, and perhaps to go to Ottawa for talks with Porsild and Dr. Jenness . . . . Made arrangements with Bob Randall for a plane to come for us on Aug. 19 or 20. It is on the regular south-bound trip of the mail plane. // *Sent out a letter home. Pulled camp together and went collecting to near end of lake.*

16 Aug — 37/56.5 BOTANICAL NOTES: Fan on south shore, second down from one directly across from camp, made of coarser materials than the camp fan. // *Karl, Pops and I climbed the canyon which seemed to have a natural bridge and cut up to near timber line by a cutbank, collecting plants en route.*

17 Aug — 44/49.5 *Numbered our plants from the 15th and 16th. Drew fungi. Made a blueberry pie.* [NOTE: Entries after this date are missing. It may mark the end of the stay at Brintnell Lake.] The Ballanca returned and took us with our equipment and plant collections back to Fort Simpson. From there we went by boat upriver to Waterways and by train back to Edmonton. Transcribed April 1995.

20 Aug — [Archie Vanhee comes in. They wait for hours for wind to shift, trying occasionally to get the plane up.] We left about 150 lbs of grub on the cache. There were about 100 lbs of flour, about 10 of bacon grease, some coffee, cheese, chocolate, yeast etc. Aso we left a small shovel and a bucksaw. We put the old canoe on the cache also, over the grub and lashed down with rope.

"Man Against the North," by Norm Thomas. 1952

It was grizzly tracks in the snow that led us up off the ice field in the fog that day. But in the end, it was the grizzly that almost killed us. It was much the same way with the river. It was the river that saved us from death by starvation, but it was the river, too, that came within an ace of taking our lives.

I remember the day we came down onto Glacier Lake. The water was cold and clear and green and fairly teemed with grayling and trout. And up beyond the lake Cathedral Peak rose gray and jagged and forbidding into an azure sky. Beyond the mountains were the icefields, and beyond the icefields an unexplored mineral belt. It seemed to us that day like a wonderful vacation with fishing in virgin lakes and hunting untrod forests.

But, even then, as we stood at the edge of the forest by the lake and watched the plane that had brought us in prepare for take-off, there was about the place an atmosphere of foreboding that we could not rid ourselves of. Here was a hard country and we did not delude ourselves that ours would be an easy job -- or, for that matter, that it could be done at all. This was the Nahanni River in the far Northwest Territories of Canada. Here so many men had met the wilderness at its worst, had grappled with it and lost to it, that the river long since had become a terrible legend up and down the North country.

We watched the plane as it circled, yellow and black, against the gray granite peak and saw the pilot waggle his wings in a final salute. We heard it drone away toward the black slate mountains along the Flat River and through some snowy pass and out across the endless bush towards the Alaska Highway.

The sound of the plane faded away. The water slapped gently against the shore. From somewhere off in the distance came the lonesome cry of a loon and up along the granite peaks was the far-away rumble of an avalanche. Then at last there was no sound at all but that of the wind and the spruce. In all the vast

Norm Thomas at Glacier Lake, 1952.

Northland for 150 miles in any direction there was no other human but the three of us.

There was also another motive behind the expedition. And that was the exploration for minerals -- particularly uranium. The aerial photography had revealed some very promising faulted structures and contact zones in a certain valley back of the ice fields. The botanical research could be done anywhere along the way but it was the mineral exploration that determined the course of the expedition.

Chosen by the Catholic University of America to conduct the exploration was Dick Shamp of Washington, DC. Shamp at that time was an aerial photo interpreter for Air Force intelligence. He was also a capable geologist. He in turn selected Howie Martyn of Yale University to make the botanical study. Martyn was also an experienced mountain climber. I was retained as photographer for the expedition.

After we left the States we had driven up the Alaska Highway to Watson lake in the Yukon Territory. There we had waited many days for an unusual low-hanging body of moist warm air to pass over and clear the mountain passes of clouds before an oldtime bush pilot named Dalziel could fly us in to our base camp at Glacier Lake.

But the plane was gone now. We watched it disappear and then we turned to meet the wilderness. Down along the lake on a grassy promontory we built a cache on top of three high poles and on the poles we put stovepipe so bears and wolverines couldn't climb up, and on the platform we put the food and equipment that we could not carry with us.

We had a lot of the Army's Arctic Trail rations. We broke these down and the bulky items such as crackers and cookies we left behind, and the compact, highly concentrated things like browned meat and cereal bars we took along. We made up our packs and when we couldn't get everything in them we cut out all but the absolutely essential equipment and what little room

A rough attempt at illustrating the Shamp/Pentagon route as sketched by
Martyn on 1:50,000 contours, the grey line running from Glacier Lake,
up Frost Creek, down Martyn Creek, up Thomas Creek to Mount
Mulholland, over a high pass and down into Bologna Creek, down
Bologna to the Nahanni River. From there, the team rafted the river to a
point above the outflow of Brintnell Creek, and then walked back to
Glacier Lake.

was left, we filled with food. The packs still weighed about 75 pounds.

We turned away from the lake and pushed off into the bush that climbed into the mountains. When I look back on it, I don't know how we stood up under those packs the first days of the trek. I didn't think then that we would go far with them, but we tried and we found that the human body could take more punishment than we had thought.

There was Dick Shamp, just out of an office in Washington. He was the biggest man among us and weighed about 200 pounds, but he was awfully soft and overweight. The over-exertion made him sick and those first days he couldn't keep his food down and almost didn't eat at all. I don't know how he kept up his strength but he kept going. The torture that he was undergoing showed clearly on his fleshy white face that was just beginning to be covered by a scraggly growth of beard. We often had to climb back down and help him with his pack those first days, and when he would catch up to us he would fall down in his tracks and lie exhausted where he fell until it was time to go on again.

But we didn't mind helping Dick and there would come a time when he would help us, for the excess flesh that he carried then was to stand him in good stead in the leaner days that followed. There were times when I think he would have given up if we had suggested it, but fortunately, there never came a time when all of us felt like throwing in the towel at the same time. And as long as there was one of us capable and willing to push on and take the lead the others followed.

And the man who most often held the lead those days was Howie Martyn. Howie was in no better condition than the rest of us because he had just come from the classrooms of Yale. He was about six feet four and thin as a rail, but he had the advantage of a pair of mighty long legs, and he knew how to strike a slow steady pace that he could hold for hours over the roughest terrain. He was a great mountaineer, too. He could pick the easiest routes and spot dangerous slide areas before we got onto them.

Howie had keen gray eyes that always held a calculating look as though he was continually estimating his chances against the wilds. He had a rather prominent and sort of hooked nose that gave him a hawk-like look. But I best remember Howie for his cigarettes. It seems now that he was always rolling a smoke with head bowed and eyes lowered under the floppy wide brim of his old yellow felt hat, or else he was smoking it down close to his finger tips in a careful effort not to waste the precious tobacco. I remember, too, that he didn't have much beard and we were always kidding him about being freshly shaven.

They were cruel days at first. We pushed ourselves until we couldn't go any farther and then we pushed a little more before we stopped. It all got to be a familiar pattern. We rolled out early in the mornings and travelled until noon and usually stopped from exhaustion. At noon we ate a meager lunch and rested a couple of hours during which time I did my writing, changed film in the cameras and did what other little jobs had to be done. In the afternoons we pushed on again until darkness was near. It got dark late during the summer that far north, so we had a lot of time to travel. But even so, we were lucky if on an average day we covered six miles as the crow would fly.

You see, it would have been hard enough just walking down a beaten trail with the heavy ski packs we had to carry. But unfortunately, there was no trail. Even game trails were scarce and not well defined and had a nasty habit of petering out completely just as we would think we had a good one for sure. Down low on the slopes and in the bottoms along the streams we had dense spruce forests with jumbled windfalls and deep moss, and where there were little streams or swales, there would be impenetrable thickets of willow and alder that grew so thick that a man many times couldn't push his way through. Higher up on the mountain sides the forests disappeared but dwarf birch grew about shoulder high and thick as a meadow.

Martyn (ahead) and Shamp making one of many creek crossings during
their expedition.

It tangled around your legs until you couldn't move ahead and sometimes, it threw you down. So you cursed and damn near cried, and then plowed on.

Up above timberline there was no brush, but there the mountains were awfully steep and there were dangerous slide areas and treacherous rocks overgrown with slippery moss so that

Mt. Sir James McBrien.

you could not see the holes between the rocks until you had already stepped in them and fallen through. There, too, were the snowfields with rotten crusts so that you could almost walk over but you never quite crossed one that you didn't suddenly drop through up to your waist and then have to struggle out dragging your pack behind you. I don't know which was the hardest to buck -- the bush or the mountains. But wherever you were at the moment, that seemed the worst.

And so the days passed one by one and we went up out of the bush and climbed the jagged frontal range back of Glacier Lake and searched for a pass into the next watershed. But there was no pass. So, we descended into a side valley and climbed again against the frontal range and that time there was a pass. It took us one whole day just to cross over. We left our sweat behind on the talus slopes and in the deep snows and descended from the pass across a risky slide area into a great glacier-carved bowl where there was a lake beginning to fill from the melting snow, and there we dropped from exhaustion and rolled into our sleeping bags where we had fallen. Dick was very ill from over-exertion.

We had crossed the pass and we came now to a world man may never have seen before. I remember that back on the talus slopes on the other side of the range we had come across an old and weathered shell from a .300 Savage and that was the last sign of human existence that we saw. It is doubtful that anyone had ever gone that way because our path led only to the big ice-fields where no one could have any reason to go -- where we should not ourselves have gone had not the aerial photography revealed something very interesting that had long been hidden to the world.

And so for two days we climbed down along a tumbling mountain stream into a great canyon amid scenery that the mind cannot imagine. Because we thought no one had ever seen it before, we gave it a name. We called it Martyn Creek after Howie. And up on one side was a great, sheer mountain capped by thick cushions of snow and because of its shape we named it the Saddle-back Mountain.

Eventually we came to another and bigger river and this we called Thomas River after the author. We made a treacherous

143

crossing of Martyn Creek and turned up Thomas River because we saw on the photography that it headed up against the ice fields. We moved off through deep moss under giant spruce where the sun never shone. We passed under a great waterfall where a side stream fell down out of the uplands and we named this stream Gold Creek because there was a fair showing of color in the sands. We had lost our gold pan off of Howie's pack sometime on the first pass and now we had to use a pie tin for panning.

I remember Gold Creek pretty well because I got a miserable ducking in its icy waters and it cost me my hat. While crossing the stream on a log I lost my balance and my pack pulled me off the log and dragged me under. The swirling flood swept me downstream until I lodged against some boulders and climbed ashore. But my hat was gone. After that I wore a battered old red alpine hat that Howie had in his pack.

It was about this time that my back gave way. We had long had bad sores where the webbing of the packs pressed against the base of our spines but now my sacroiliac had slipped out of joint right at that point and the weight of the pack became almost unbearable. Howie and Dick took on some of my load and we pushed on to the base of the glacier that led up to the ice field.

We made our camp that night at the last scrubby clump of brush that afforded twigs for a fire. It was high on a steep rocky hillside at the head of the valley and we had to pile rocks on the lower side of our sleeping bags so we wouldn't roll down the hill that night. We couldn't see the glacier yet from that point but the river disappeared under ice and snow that filled a narrow defile which wound up around a mountain and we knew that the glacier lay just back of the mountain.

Up until now we had had more or less fair weather and there was no indication of any change when we went to bed that night. We slept restlessly on our sharply tilted bed of rocks and prepared to roll out early the next morning because that was the day that would spell success or failure for the expedition. For that day we would have to climb the glacier, cross the ice field, and find a pass through the mountains to the next watershed -- to the head of the valley we had named the Dogleg because of its shape on our aerial photo-map. There might not be a pass that we could negotiate. We couldn't tell for sure from the aerial photography. But we had gambled everything on there being one. In any case, whether we succeeded or failed, it would be a hard day for all of us.

Now, at this crucial moment, fate played a cruel trick on us. We awoke that morning to the slow steady beat of rain on our sleeping bags. And we looked out on a bleak wet world where heavily saturated clouds hung dark and threatening in the valley and hid the mountains in ominous swirling vapor. We crawled reluctantly out of our bags and huddled among the boulders beside a pitiful little fire made from wet twigs. We ate the morning meal in gloomy silence and allowed ourselves a little more than our usual meager ration because of what we knew lay ahead of us that day.

After breakfast we waterproofed our boots with dubbin to protect them as much as possible from the snow we would be wading in all day. It was then I noticed that the soles were about to come off my boots. Actually they were not my boots at all but an old pair of engineering boots that I had gotten from Howie, several sizes too big for me so that I had to wear two pairs of heavy wool socks and a pair of moccasins to fill them up. My own boots that I had worn in had turned out to have rotten welts and had come apart while we were still at the base camp. Now I could picture myself staggering along in broken down feet wrapped in rags. It was hard enough to walk under that pack as it was. I didn't comment on the situation at the time but squirmed into my pack and started off after Howie who was already an indistinct black blob on a field of white snow that led up through the gorge toward the glacier.

The river cascaded down through the gorge underneath the snow that we were walking on, and every now and then we came to holes in the snow through which we could see the frothing water and we skirted these with great care lest we slip and slide into the river and be carried under the ice. The rain kept falling without letup and our black nylon slickers were wet and shiny and startlingly black against the snow. It was with difficulty that I protected the camera from the rain as I photographed the dismal scene that surrounded us. Gradually the dampness and the chill seeped into our bones.

Sometime about mid-morning we came to the bottom of a high, pyramidal moraine which curved gently and climbed for a mile or two up to the foot of an ugly black mountain. The crevasse-scarred tongues of two great glaciers licked out along each side of the moraine. The glacier on our left climbed high up into an impregnable range of mountains and the one on our right swept out and up in a series of ice banks that were blue-gray under the dull sky and led out onto the big ice field.

We climbed the steep side of the moraine over black rocks that were wet and slippery from the rain. We walked along the crest of the moraine and climbed steadily to the bottom of the black mountain that separated the two glaciers. There obviously was no way over the mountains to our left so we decided to strike out across the edge of the ice field to our right. We ate a clammy, cold lunch before we left the moraine. It was still raining.

Down on the glacier were great crevasses. To avoid these we skirted along the edge of the ice field on the steeply sloping snow base at the foot of the mountain. Howie Martyn led off slowly, meticulously stamping out steps across the snow slope. Dick and I waited on the moraine until Howie was just a black spot on a field of white and then we followed more swiftly in his steps.

Howie came to a rock slide out along the snow base and there he rested until Dick and I came up to him. We slumped on the wet cold rocks and looked down into the black void out of which we had climbed and out of that void we saw the fog moving in -- creeping, swirling, enveloping the black mountains in a gray blanket of nothingness. It came up across the glaciers along the moraine to the mountain and out along the snow base until it swallowed us and on out across the icefield.

We got up and started on soon because it was too miserable to rest long on the wet rocks. We were getting very tired now and stiff from the cold. Dick took the lead. Somewhere nearby we heard an avalanche rumble down across our backtrail but we could see nothing in the fog. The mountain on our left was lost to our view. The ice field on our right blended into the whiteness of the atmosphere so that one could not tell where the ice left off and the fog began.

Men in hooded black nylon slickers were very dark in the swirling white, yet a hundred feet away they became lost to view, and at such times one felt very much alone and hurried faster to catch up with the others.

How long we went on like that I don't know. We got to be kind of numb to time and space. And for what? What if there was no pass through the mountains off the ice field into the Dogleg? And, if there was a pass how would we ever find it in that soup? We went on.

Then up off the ice and snow a track crossed our path. The wind of the night before had drifted it over with snow so that we couldn't tell what animal had left the trail. We turned and went along with it. We began to climb -- gradually at first; then steeper. Sometime later, just how much later it was I don't know, a black outcrop of rock loomed up out of the whiteness. And when we reached it we found it was at the top of a pass.

We fell down with our packs on the rocks that were wet and cold but very welcome and we rested there until the chill began to seep into our bones and stiffen our muscles. We got up and then started down out of the pass. It was then we noticed the tracks leading off the rocks were no longer drifted over with snow but were sharp and clear now and very big. The tracks we had followed up off the ice field to the pass that we might not otherwise have found were those of a giant grizzly.

Dick Shamp, who carried our only heavy rifle, moved off in the lead. Howie stopped and took out of his pack a short-barrelled .22 Hornet Air Force survival rifle with a collapsable stock. I too had carried one of these at first, but when a shell exploded in the chamber and jammed there, rendering the gun useless, I abandoned it, and now I undid the flap of my pistol holster and swung it around into a more accessible position. We had found that the one thing in the North that wins the unanimous and hearty respect of all experienced bushmen is the grizzly. We had absorbed a little of that respect. We would absorb a lot more.

We staggered off down the snow slope and skirted a small frozen pond, still following the tracks, and climbed another slope. It was then the fog opened up before us and there at our feet was the deepest, blackest hole in the earth that one might well imagine. The bleak, glacier-scarred terrain fell away in endless rocky benches until the bottom of the pit was lost in swirling mist.

This was the destination we had fought to reach. Somewhere down in this black hole was the mineral belt that we had set out to explore. This was what we called the valley of the Dogleg. We stood for a long time there on the precipice trying to grasp the immensity of the scene before us. After the whiteness of the ice field, the blackness of the rain-drenched earth was startling. There was something eerie about that vapor-draped cauldron. Out across the canyon and up toward the other ice field we counted at least ten different glaciers. One was a tremendous thing that seemed to fill the whole upper end of the valley.

Howie moved his foot and disloged a stone that clattered down over the rock ledges and that seemed to break the spell that had held us there. We moved off over rocks that were slippery and treacherous from the rain. Here on the stone benches the grizzly tracks no longer showed and we more or less forgot about the bear. Clinging to the face of the cliff and looking for the easiest way down occupied all of our attention. We were conscious only of the misery that we felt from the wet and cold and of our desire to get to the bottom of the gorge and find firewood for the night.

Howie was in the lead. We had lowered him down onto another ledge, and, not finding an immediate descent to the bench below, he had edged along the shelf to our left and disappeared around a cornice of rock. I was helping Dick down when we heard him yell. His cry, half of fear and half of warning, was followed closely by a shot. Just the one shot and no more. Dick looked at me and we knew without speaking what had happened. I was lying flat on my stomach with both of my hands grasping Dick's wrist. He was feeling with his toes for a foothold on the ledge below. He found his footing and I let go of his wrist and handed down his rifle.

Dick grabbed the gun and hurried off, clumsily under his pack and not too carefully, along the ledge. I slipped out of my own pack and sprang to the ledge below. Dick had disappeared around the cornice and now I heard the heavy thunder of the 30.06. My own pistol was in my hand as I advanced along the shelf. Then I saw Dick stagger back around the cornice. He was backing up hurriedly and once he stumbled and almost fell. Then there was the grizzly almost on him but having some trouble getting his immense bulk around the cornice due to the narrowness of the ledge. It gave Dick just enough time to get set and he fired again -- point blank this time. I pumped a couple of shots from my pistol but I doubt if they had any effect. But Dick's shot was enough because the big animal shied away to its left and fell as it did so, plunging to its death on the ledge below.

I ran past Dick. I could see that he wasn't hurt. I darted around the cornice and brought up short. Howie wasn't there.

"Howie," I yelled. And I was deathly afraid there would be no answer.

149

But the answer came. "Down here," he called.

I whirled around and looked down and saw Howie sprawled out under his pack on the bench below, and about twenty feet away was the dead grizzly.

"Are you hurt?" I said.

"Just got the wind knocked out of me."

Howie, it turned out, had come face to face with the bear and had fired on instinct with the .22. The bullet had probably bounced off the grizzly's head just making him mad. The Hornet hadn't fired again because the shell had blown up in the chamber and jammed as mine had done earlier. Howie had jumped to the ledge below just as Dick got into the fight. But it left us now with only the rifle and my pistol.

Darkness was closing in. We left the dead grizzly where it fell and hurried on down over the benches that had been scooped out by glaciers many centuries ago. Not until we reached the very bottom of the valley did we find any willows on a spot of high ground surrounded by marsh. With a good deal of trouble we managed to get a fire going and dried out our water-soaked clothing. It was still raining.

We had discovered by this time that we were all very weak and that we were getting weaker by the day. "Tomorrow we'll lay over and rest up," Dick said.

All that night it rained and the nylon tents leaked as usual and the rubberized bottoms held in the water and soaked the down bags so that after a couple of hours we were too cold to sleep any more that night. Nor did the rain stop the next day and the clouds never rose out of the eerie black depths of the valley.

Our morale was low like the clouds that hung over us. We were very listless and we knew that our ration was failing to keep up our strength. Our sole food, day after day, was for breakfast; one half of an ounce-and-a-half cereal bar, and a small hotcan that had been skinned out of its heating unit to make for lighter packing. These consisted mostly of ham and eggs which had seemed to have more body than the other hotcan rations but which now proved too rich for our systems, and we found that we couldn't force it down without gagging. For lunch each man had one half of a five-ounce ground meat bar which he crumbled into half a canteen cup of green pea soup and cooked to make a rich and filling gruel. To go with that he had a half cup of cocoa. For the evening meal he had the other half of his lunch ration. We had counted on some game, but we had seen hardly any game since leaving Glacier Lake. There had been no fish in the high, cold, muddy glacier streams that we had been on.

That day Dick hunted out of camp a little way up toward the big glacier but saw no sign of game. We thought of going up after a leg of the grizzly that we had killed the night before, but no one felt like he had the strength for the climb even if he could have found the place again in the clouds that hung down into the valley.

The next day it was still drizzling rain but we had to go on now regardless of the weather. Although we were in the Dogleg and headed downstream we were still traveling directly away from our base and would continue to do so until we reached the bend of the river that formed the Dogleg. There was no turning back now. After we had crossed the ice field we knew that we had burned our bridges behind us because we would never have had the strength to climb back over those passes. There was nothing to do but follow the stream down to the river. We packed up and moved out.

First I went with Dick up the valley a little way to a high ridge where I could photograph the big glacier. Howie didn't go because his feet were so badly broken down and painful that it was pure torture to take an unnecessary step. Later that day we started down the Dogleg and had to buck dwarf birch and willow brush that was so thick it was all but impossible to push our way through. At times we became so discouraged and maddened that we could have cried.

Eventually we came to a grove of spruce that bordered the Dogleg and behind the spruce was a waterfall and up on the high benches above the waterfall was a lake. It was in the vicinity of the lake that the faulted area lay that we were most interested in exploring for minerals. We decided to cross the Dogleg and camp in the spruce grove and the next day begin the exploration.

We had waded these mountain streams many times before so we didn't give much thought to this particular one until Dick had started across and suddenly discovered that the water was too deep and too swift. He turned back just in time and we hauled him out onto the bank. We looked for a wider, shallower spot and still foresaw no trouble. Dick started across again and Howie was so sure of an easy crossing that he waded in too. I prepared to follow but suddenly, out of the corner of my eye, I saw the current sweep Dick off his feet and the heavy pack dragged him under almost immediately. I ran to his aid but the current swept him along faster than I could run. The river rolled him over and over and smashed him against some big boulders and finally deposited him in a shallows on the opposite side. I watched him crawl out onto the bank and lie there a minute and then get up and stagger back into the stream for his rifle. Then he went off in search of firewood. I could see that he was blue and knew he must be nearly frozen. Howie had made it back to shore and I went up to him.

We conferred and decided to chop down a tall spruce tree so that it would fall across the river and we could then cross on it. We had only one little hand axe so it took some time to fell thetree and when it did fall, it was just a little short, and the current immediately carried it off down stream. There was nothing left now but to wade it. I left my pack behind and crossed on the downstream side of Howie so that he could brace against me with his pack and in that manner we crossed to within a few feet of the other side before the stream washed Howie down. But Dick had come over to the edge of the river and he dashed in just in time to grab him and save him. A little later we discovered a small spruce already across the river a little downstream, but it was rotten and slippery and sagged so much just under body-weight we didn't dare risk it with packs of valuable gear.

It was decided then that I would cross back to the other side and not risk bringing my pack over with the valuable camera equipment, but that I would camp over there until Dick and Howie had conducted the explorations and then we would proceed downstream until we found a more suitable spot to join forces. We thought it best for me not to climb with them up to the faulted area since my boot soles were almost gone and I had better conserve what was left.

So there were campfires on both sides of the Dogleg that night, and it was very lonesome on my side of the river. I ate and turned in early and slept fitfully. It was still raining. The next morning I watched as Howie and Dick climbed the mountain beside the waterfall and disappeared onto the high, mossy benches. Later on, I hunted along the river bottom with my pistol but found no game. In the afternoon a storm moved in and hid the uplands in cloud. Along toward dusk the boys returned to camp and I crossed over to see what they had found.

It turned out that they had climbed from bench to bench that never seemed to end and Dick had given out finally, so Howie went on alone. At last Howie reached the lake but by then there was a snow storm raging around him so he turned back. They had found and explored some of the faults that had lured us there in the first place and found them to contain little sign of mineralization.

But our disappointment with this was the least of our worries that night. We had all done a lot of thinking that day and it had come to us with shocking clarity just what a spot we were really in. Dick's experience with the river the night before had been a very serious blow to us. Not only had it brought home to us the grim reality of the struggle we were engaged in against the untamed forces of nature, but it also cost us two cameras, our only Geiger counter and our last remaining rifle. Both Dick and Howie's cameras had gotten drenched in the muddy water and no longer worked. The Geiger counter had gotten wet and perhaps banged against a boulder too because it was completely dead. Dick's rifle had the breach smashed against the boulder and broken. That left us with only one firearm, my pistol, and there were only a handful of shells for it. These we would have to save in case of an encounter with a grizzly. My boots were about gone. All of our feet were badly broken down and Dick had fractured a kneecap and his collarbone when smashed against boulders in the river. We were all very weak and listless and growing more so by the day.

We became abruptly aware, for the first time, of the peril we were faced with. We put out of our minds all thought of further exploration that might take us out of our way or delay us. From that time on all thought and every ounce of energy was directed solely toward getting away with our lives.

We broke camp and struck out early the next morning. We hadn't moved ten feet in the waterlogged bush before we were wet to the bone, slickers not withstanding. It was the fifth straight day of rain and that day it was raining harder than usual. There was no sign of letup. We were still separated. Dick and Howie were on the left side of the river and I was on the right. They had the easier trail and I was often out of contact with them for hours at a time. I fought hard against the bush and the mountainsides I had to climb, and was almost about to drop when I again came into sight of my companions about noon. There was a wide shallows at that point and they waded across to join me. I was never so happy to have companionship. Howie had gotten caught in quicksand that morning and Dick had dragged him out. I couldn't help thinking what if it had been me, alone as I was.

The valley down which we were traveling got wider that afternoon but the trail became no easier because now we had vast moose meadows, or swamps, to cross and many times we waded waist deep in the sloughs. That night we had trouble finding solid ground to pitch camp. I guess that day and night saw our spirits reach their lowest ebb. For five days now we had not seen the sun and the rain had not stopped. It was as though fate had decreed that as long as we were on the Dogleg it should not cease to storm. It seemed like nature had marshaled all her forces against us. So overwhelming were these forces that we sometimes felt like throwing ourselves on the ground and crying.

The night was little less miserable than the day. The rain beat at our tents and soaked our sleeping bags. We lay in the dark and shivered and our bones ached from the cold. Sometimes during the night one of the boys developed a fitful coughing and I got to thinking about pneumonia and what would happen if one of us came down with it. I didn't sleep any more that night. I thought about the people back home and how I would like to be with my little boy and of all the things I had done and of all the things I had wanted to do but hadn't done. Somehow, sometime, the night dragged to a miserable end.

It was the Fourth of July. We nooned that day at the bend of the Dogleg where it turned back toward the Nahanni river and our base camp. And while we were stopped the sun came out. We couldn't have celebrated the fourth more joyously. Still we couldn't help thinking of other Fourths when we had been at the beach with hotdogs and hamburgers to eat and the sun beating down on us and cold beer to drink.

Then one day about dusk we came down out of the mountains to the Nahanni river and found it wide and deep and, though moving very fast, we believed it was raftable. We were very weak from malnutrition and hardly able to carry our packs. It was still a good seventy-five miles to our base at Glacier Lake and only a scant ten days before our rendezvous with the plane.

Dick Shamp putting the finishing touches on the raft that took the
expedition from the mouth of Bologna Creek to a gravel bar in the
middle of the South Nahanni River some twenty miles away.

Even when we had been strong we were lucky if we made six miles a day through the jungle-like bush. And now we could hardly move at all. We decided to build a raft and take our chances with the river. We pitched our camp on a sandy beach just as the regular evening shower came upon us.

The very next morning we set about building a raft. We had only one small hand axe, but with this we cut spruce trees out of the forest a little way back from the river. Trees that were already down were waterlogged and rotten and green logs were too heavy so we concentrated on trees that were dead and cured but still standing. We chopped these into ten-foot lengths and dragged them to the riverbank. We were so weakened that it took the greatest effort of the will to make our bodies perform the slightest movement. So it was with slow and torturous labor that we finally assembled enough logs for the raft. It was then our plans received an unbearable jolt.

We had brought along a length of cotton rope with which to lash a raft together in case we found a raftable river. Only the day before we had used the rope as a safety measure while crossing a mountain stream. Now Dick looked in his pack for the rope. He looked a long time and at last he said very apologetically that the rope was gone. We looked at each other and each knew what the other was thinking, but we said nothing at all. We went to our packs and rummaged through them and gathered everything that could possibly serve us as lashing. When we had finished our pile included bootlaces, belts, fishing line, wire snares, pack straps and various odds and ends. Still, there was not enough to lash every log in its place. So, to conserve lashings, we built the raft by first laying out two heavy main members and notching them, then binding the cross members to them, one at each end and one in the middle. Then we filled in with cross logs, laid in loosely without lashing. To hold the latter in place, we bound two poles over them, one on each side of the raft, and tied them down at each end.

The raft was ready by mid-afternoon. We ate lunch but without much appetite. None of us knew what lay ahead on the big river. None of us had ever built a raft before or tried to handle one on a river. We didn't know if the crude affair would even float us and our equipment or if it would hold together at all. We didn't know if we could steer it or guide it in any way. The river was big and deep and ice cold, and I for one couldn't swim and had always had a certain fear of deep water. Dick and Howie could swim, but it probably wouldn't do them much good in that strong current and the numbing cold water.

Everything that was important or valuable - the camera equipment and exposed film, our notebooks, the more compact elements of our remaining food supply, the pistol and one sleeping bag - we put into one pack which we determined to hang onto at all costs, even though we had to let the other packs go.

We piled our gear on the raft and with what seemed like our last ounce of strength, we pried the raft off the bar where we had built it and into the river. The current seized it immediately and was much stronger than we had thought. We scrambled madly to get aboard before it was swept away. We had launched on the outside of a big bend and now we found the current pressing us against the bank so that we couldn't get out into the stream. Down ahead near the bend was a big boulder with the water pouring over it. For an unhappy minute we thought that was the end of our beginning. But somehow we scraped over the top of the rock without breaking apart. We had cut fifteen-foot saplings to use as push poles, but they did little good since the river was too deep for poling. So we just ricocheted helplessly along the shoreline.

At last we were swept out into the stream and I put to use a big rudder that I had made by tying a pack board to a forked sapling. But since we were moving at the same speed as the current, we couldn't get any steerage. But later we found that by applying the pack board like a big oar, we could direct the cumbersome craft so as to avoid dangerous obstacles provided we could spot the hazard far enough ahead to give us time to work. In this way we avoided any dangers.

For several hours the river was wide and straight and not too fast. We relaxed a little and laughed some and broke out a package of hard candy and a meat bar. We thought at that time we really had it made.

I guess we were still thinking that when up ahead we heard a loud roaring sound. It was very faint at first and then it got louder and then we could see white water. We saw that if we could keep to the inside of the bend, we could miss the worst part of the rapids and we worked hard on the big oar. But the current was against us and when we saw we were fighting a losing battle, we gave up and just watched and waited.

"We're heading right for the worst part," Dick said.

"Get down low and hang on," Howie said.

Then we were in the middle of it. One second we were swallowed in a deep trough that we couldn't get out of and the next second we were flung high on the crest of a great wave.

"We're going to hit that cliff sure as hell," Dick screamed above the thunder of the rapids.

I remember that we all stood up on the pitching deck and then moved toward the front and stood there with poles poised like knights with lances ready to meet the danger. At that moment the river smashed us hard against the face of the cliff. With our feet braced, we tried to absorb some of the shock through the poles that we held, but they might as well have been toothpicks for all the good they did. One corner of the raft struck the rocks with a tremendous thud that knocked us all into the water, and while we scrambled to get on our feet there was a terrible rending and grinding sound and we knew then that the raft was breaking up. The force of the current held us pinned against the cliff for one long terrible moment while the raft slowly disintegrated, log by log, and we fought with what little strength we had left to hang on to something. One moment would find us on top of a log, but the next moment would see us plunged again up to our necks in the icy water. After what seemed like an eternity, we broke clear of the cliff and were caught up again in the plunging rapids. It was a continuing battle to hang onto what wreckage we could. I succeeded at last in getting three or four logs together between my legs and riding on top of them. Howie was immersed up to his chin in the churning water and two logs rested over his shoulders so he couldn't climb out. I could reach out and touch him and try to hang onto him, but couldn't otherwise help him. Up ahead of us Dick was having trouble. No sooner would he get on top of a log than it would go under and throw him once again into the raging water where he would begin the same uphill struggle all over again.

Once during the mile or more that we must've been carried through the rapids, we passed a moose standing unconcernedly in the edge of the river watching us go by. I remember some-one saying he wished to hell he could change places with the moose right now. And once I heard Dick ask Howie how he was making out.

"Okay," Howie said. "But I can't hold out much longer. I'm getting numb."

Once Dick was flung loose from the wreckage and fought hard to reach us. I watched with a sinking sensation without being able to help.

Then all at once we found ourselves in shallow water scraping along over some boulders that wrenched our legs between the logs, and which we now seemed unable to get untangled from. We were at the head of a bar in the middle of the river and somehow we managed to get loose from the wreckage before it broke loose and was swept on by. We dragged two packs out with us, but one was carried away with the wreck.

We were already blue from the cold and almost numb. Hastily we built a fire of driftwood and it was quite some time before we could talk without our teeth chattering. Then we looked about us and sized up our immediate situation. There were no trees on the bar but there was some driftwood and we counted the logs in sight and figured there were enough to build another raft. That would be our only way off the island since we were in the middle of the river with rapids pouring down on either side of us, and even that was a risky chance because the rapids plunged straight down against another cliff where the river turned abruptly and disappeared behind a timbered point of land. There was no telling what lay just out of sight.

We slept restlessly in shifts because there were only two sleeping bags for the three of us. I sat up the first watch and huddled by the fire behind a pile of driftwood as the evening rains came and the cold wind swept down out of the gorge.

When it was light, we began work on another raft, a cruder affair this time because now we could not select our logs but had to use what was on hand. We had no more lashings so we ripped one of the nylon tents into strips about six inches wide and used these to bind the logs together. When this was done we tried to launch the raft off the side of the bar where we had built it but it was too heavy and took us several hours of back-breaking work before it floated.

As the current once more took us in tow, I imagine that our thoughts must have been pretty much the same - something like "here goes nothing." But we somehow managed to avoid the cliff at the end of the chute and came a short while later into smooth water.

Our second raft lasted just about two hours. And then there came a time when down ahead we saw an island and at the head of the island a great log jam. I plied the big oar in an effort to swing us to the right with the main channel. But there was a strong cross current that pulled us to the left toward a fast, shallow channel, so that in the end we swept head-on against the log jam. We hit with a tremendous impact, and the pressure of the water immediately turned the raft on end and pressed it vertically against the jam. We struggled out over the top onto the logs and watched helplessly as our second pack floated on by just out of our reach. With it went the one remaining nylon tent, that we might have used for lashings, and another sleeping bag.

For awhile we thought we might salvage the raft intact, but when our efforts proved fruitless we took it apart log by log and saved the nylon bindings which were now so precious. That night we slept in shifts again, but they were shorter shifts now because there was only one bag for the three of us, and it was raining again as usual. That was the way it would be from there on out.

Moreover, we had only one cooking utensil between us and that was a canteen cup. Our only ration now was meat bar crumbled in a cup of green pea soup, which made a rather palatable, filling gruel. We took turns eating from the cup as it was passed around.

The next morning we reassembled the raft and again experienced trouble launching it from the high bank. At last we were afloat again though this time the raft was very loose and there were wide spaces between the logs that our legs kept slipping through. But somehow we kept it together and slowly the miles of river passed beneath us.

It was a cloudy day and since our watches had long since been destroyed and we could not see the sun, it was hard to tell what time it was getting to be. But it must have been close to dusk when down ahead we again heard that all too familiar sound of rapids. The water that we were in at the moment was very slow and we thought we could pull ashore to investigate. But when we tried, we found that we had waited too long. The current already had us.

We knew from our photo map that the river forked at that point and we thought maybe the sound we heard was just that of the other stream coming in. But when we were almost on it, we saw that the sound was caused by the river pouring over the top of a big rock about the size of a house that was in the river about twenty feet off shore. We appeared to be heading right for it. It was plain to see now that if we went over the rock we would have had it because the water going over the rock was like water going over the top of a dam. Then at the last moment the cross current of the other fork swept us past the rock between it and the bank. We narrowly avoided being caught in the backwash, then rode out a series of rapids below the rock and breathed easy again.

We discovered now that the river was bigger and much faster and more powerful than it had been above the forks. Our oar had no effect against the current here. However, the river was cut into many channels, some of which were very shallow but fast and when we got into these, the raft hung up on boulders and the bindings snapped, and when we broke loose we had to fight like mad to tie the raft together before the same thing happened all over again.

Darkness was almost on us now. Our feet had been in the icy water all day and now they were almost numb from the cold. When we tried to get ashore, we found we were helpless in this fast current. We began to be worried that darkness would catch us on the river. Then we had a stroke of luck. The river swept us close to shore and we narrowly missed a big rock at the edge of the stream, but got caught in the backwash behind the rock. We were in a sort of whirlpool now and easily got to the bank of the river. Now we found we had nothing with which to tie the raft up to shore. This problem was solved by taking enough bindings from the raft to tie one end of a push pole to the raft and the other end to a tree on the bank.

Next morning we got aboard and pushed off only to be swept around in a big arc and right back to shore again. We were in the whirlpool. For two hours we tried every trick in the bag without success. Finally a big whirl flung us far enough out that the current caught us and we were on our way.

That afternoon proved to be a nightmare beyond description. Never was there a moment's rest. We hurtled through narrow channels that twisted like a snake, though forests of spruce that had been undercut and fallen in the river to form a menace called "sweepers" in the North. We catapulted from bank to bank and sweeper to sweeper. Sometimes we rode over the sweepers and sometimes we scraped underneath, but always they tore at the raft and the bindings snapped and at such times it was only with frantic work and quite a bit of luck that we managed to hold the raft together.

In such a manner we ran the river around the foot of the Vampire Peaks and came in due time to a smooth stretch of channel on the right side of the river and in that moment, before the current could catch us again, we made the decision to abandon ship and pull hard for shore.

We were still a long way from Glacier Lake. But we knew that we could walk the rest of the way whereas on the river every bend in the channel held a new danger.

The relentless nervous tension to which we had been subjugated these past days had told on all of us. I will never forget the haunted look in Dick Shamp's eyes that day as we abandoned the raft on a mud bank under some tall birch trees. The man who had been fleshy and soft at the start of the trip was now lean and emaciated. His face was bearded and his eyes were deep sunk and tortured.

Howie Martyn, too, showed the strain. He seldom smiled anymore and he smoked all the time - and stared with a far-off thoughtful look in his eyes.

From the raft we took enough nylon bindings to tie our remaining possessions to our backs and walked up through the bush from the river toward the shoulder of the mountain beyond which was Glacier Lake. Dick slogged along favoring his bad leg, and Howie limped slowly on broken down feet clad only in moccasins. All that afternoon we walked and when night came so came an icy rain that lasted half the night. We pushed on through the soaking bush and sometime around midnight we came down to the lake and found our cache. But the rains had come to stay and it was another ten days before the plane could get through the pass to take us out.

But one day soon we were winging out over the bush toward the black slate mountains and below was a twisting river ribbon that was the Nahanni river - the river that had almost conquered us, but that in the end had saved us.

From "TERRAIN CONDITIONS CORRELATED WITH VEGETATION ON SUBARCTIC AND ARCTIC MOUNTAINS, DEDUCIBLE FROM AIR AND GROUND PHOTOS," by DICK SHAMP

Test Location: South Nahanni Valley, NWT, Canada

In this section comprising Plates M-1 to M-30, there is illustrated a mountainous region of relatively recent elevation, showing the rugged topography and steep slopes characteristic of "young" mountains.

As in mountainous regions anywhere in the world, the principal influence affecting travel conditions is the steep slope of much of the earth's surface, while water-level assumes a very secondary role. This is exactly the opposite of travel conditions in the lowlands where slopes is a very secondary influence and water-table of prime importance.

Vegetation modifies travel conditions for better or worse in mountains more than in lowlands. Thus, a stand of alders is always associated with wet soil. On steep slopes the alders are practically an impossible barrier to travel upward and greatly increase the difficulty caused by the slope. But on lowlands the same alders have a much smaller modifying effect, although the soil is equally wet in both areas.

A rough idea of the extent of the mountains in the arctic and subarctic regions of USSR is shown on Map 6, the last section of this report. The information shown and explained on the following thirty plates can be used as an introductory study in the photo-interpretation of the vegetation on these mountains. The parallel is likely to be closest between the vegetation on the mountains of Kamchatka and the Nahanni Valley, at least as regards the masses of vegetation. Both are regions of recent uplift as shown by the presence of hot springs, the very steep slopes, etc.

From a military standpoint, it seems safe to consider such mountains as an impassible barrier to an army until a substantial road has been built across them. The photo-interpretation of vegetation is likely to be of little use to the engineer in laying out such roads. But from another military standpoint, that of small reconnaissance parties or small detachments, the mountains of the arctic and subarctic are passable. It is for this purpose that the following plates have been prepared. From the present study and the general information accumulated by our Arctic Institute the following generalizations have been laid down for the photo-interpretation of this and other mountains of similar climate:

1. In general, detachments larger than reconnaissance parties will find the most practical routes of travel in the larger valleys and across the relatively few passes. Vegetation in the valleys is a fair indicator of the travel conditions there as shown in the following plates.

2. Small Reconnaissance and/or scouting parties will find the best travel routes in such mountains to be game trails. [For each item, 2-15, Shamp refers the reader to the relevant plates]

3. Such game trails follow the line of ridges or the relatively even ground on the sides of slopes. If the valleys are relatively wide and flat, these trails will follow the banks of streams. Be it noted that moose trails often terminate at marshes and bogs, but caribou, mountain goats and sheep trails stay entirely in drier ground.

4. The top of the ridges of medial moraines, although relatively uncommon, are good routes of travel.

5. Braided streams are good routes of travel although frequent fordings to cross and recross the stream channels are necessary. Braided streams in themselves indicate the place where the slope is less than the rushing torrent that feeds them.

Lake Trout and Shamp, forty pounds lighter, back at Glacier Lake and eager to eat.

6. White spruce forests on the banks of streams or the lower slopes of the mountains, indicate good travel routes, free of obstructive underbrush and relatively dry terrain.

7. Birch-covered slopes with bushes not taller than waist-high affort the best and driest means of ascending slopes.

8. In contrast, slopes covered with willows and alders are the wettest and worst routes of ascent and descent especially in "draws."

9. Large boulders and flat rock surfaces covered with reindeer moss, offer a slippery hazard footing wherever they occur.

10. A spruce forest recently burnt over, is soon filled with a dense growth of willows which with the fallen dead branches makes a very obstructive thicket.

11. On the other had a spruce forest killed by flooding indicates deep mud.

12. Black spruce-larch forests indicate swamps and poor travel conditions.

13. In some streams it is possible to travel by rafts where the current is not too swift.

14. Rock slides or talus slopes should be ascended at an oblique angle. The amount and height of the vegetation on such slopes is an indication of the stability of such a slope. Total absence of vegetation indicates an actively sliding slope to be avoided.

15. In general glaciers, especially when snow-covered, are to be avoided unless there is at hand suitable equipment.

This spring was abnormally late. The glaciers which ordinarily begin to melt rapidly about June 15, were delayed this year at least two weeks. The seasonal aspect, especially the color of the early foliage, was correspondingly retarded, a fact that would show on color much more plainly than on black and white photography.

The ground photographs used in this series of Plates M-1 to M-30 were all taken by Norman Thomas for Richard Shamp (in whose file the negatives are kept). Howell Martyn is responsible for a considerable part of the notes on the terrain.

[A. Shamp inserts here a photo of his aerial photos laid out in a panorama of the Glacier Lake - Bologna Creek - Nahanni River area. The expedition route is marked out.

B. Next appears an aerial photo of the headwaters of Bologna Creek, location 62 degrees N, 128 degrees W approx. Stereo Panachromatic Air Vertical Photo, 1/20,000 approx. Royal Canadian Air Force A-12270-90. For all his aerial photos, Shamp provides the Canadian Air Force number. On this photo, he identifies with symbols scrub birch, granite, reddish shale, grayish shale, snow, willow, reindeer moss, and white spruce. Photos by Thomas follow with the symbols attached so interpreters can see air photo features at close range.

C. Next, Shamp presents an aerial photo of Frost Creek beside five of Thomas's ground photos, with symbols attached.

D. Aerial photo of Glacier Lake with seven ground photos (including a spectacular one of Harrison-Smith).

E. Aerial photo of the east end of Glacier Lake and Brintnell Lake, with ground photos.

F. A tributary of Bologna Creek, aerial and ground photos showing retreating glaciers and moraine.

G. What Shamp calls Martyn Creek and Thomas Creek (un-named on the contours, they join and flow into the Nahanni behind Mt. Sir James McBrien), aerial and ground photos showing tree lines and bush lines, dense willow, talus, snow bridges. Photos at the junction of the two creeks show Martyn crossing the creeks, and Martyn and Shamp camped.

George Dalziel, feeding his hungry customers, Glacier Lake, July 1952.

H. A number of aerial and ground photo comparisons along Bologna Creek dealing with distinguishing between reindeer moss and snow.

I. Aerial photo of the junction of Bologna Creek and the South Nahanni River. Ground photos show a recent burn around the Island Lakes on the Nahanni's opposite shore.

J. Ground photos of game trails along Bologna Creek and Nahanni River.

K. Aerial and ground photos of Brintnell Creek flowing out of Brintnell Glacier.

[The above alphabetical listings omit a few duplicate location aerial and ground photo comparisons, dedicated to showing different features]

H. Snyder Expedition - Upper South Nahanni River, August 1952, by Donald R. Flook

This report covers Col. H. Snyder's expedition to the upper South Nahanni River in August, 1952. The writer accompanied the expedition as observer representing the Canadian Wildlife Service.

The expedition was based during a 25-day period at Brintnell Lake . . . .

This lake, which is known locally as Glacier lake, is shown on the eight mile to one inch topographic sheets. It is described geographically, geologically, and botanically by H. M. Raup (1947).

[Flook uses Raup's book to describe the various features of the lake and its environs. He refers to Brintnell Creek as Rapids River]

Outline of Expedition

On August 2, 1952, the Snyder party arrived at Fort Simpson, having flown from Hay River by Associated Airways chartered aircraft. The party consisted of Col. H. Snyder, Mrs. Snyder, Mr. W. Griffith, Dr. H. Jennings, and Col. Snyder's 13-year-old nephew Paul Dudeck, all of Calgary; Mr. Glen Kilgour of Bearberry, Alberta, who was engaged as cook and general handyman for the trip; and the writer. All flying for the expedition was done by Associated Airways pilot Mr. R. Page, using a Bellanca aircraft.

The party and equipment were flown from Fort Simpson to Brintnell Lake in four trips - two on August 4, and two on August 5. The writer traveled on the second trip on August 4, which was flown on a direct course across the mountains from Fort Simpson.

August 4 - The camp was set up on the site of Snyder's 1937 camp on the north shore of the lake near its west end, and in the

Kraus in First Canyon. Photo by Donald Flook, 1952.

evening I set a 75-foot nylon gill net in the shallow water close to the lake shore.

August 5 - I lifted the fish net in the morning taking 15 grayling and six lake trout. In the afternoon Mr. Griffith and I rowed down the lake about two miles in the collapsible dinghy, looking over the mountain slopes adjacent to the lake.

August 6 - Kilgour and I climbed the steep slope north of the lake, following Frost Creek. After reaching the hanging valley of Frost Creek we followed the ridge east of the valley up to about 5,500 feet elevation, then returned to the creek bottom and followed it northward to its source. Occasional bear scats were observed all along the way. Moose pellets were observed scattered over the entire route, most numerously among the dwarf birch and willow of Frost Creek above timberline. Two shed moose antlers were found along the creek. One bull moose was observed in a draw high above timberline and was stalked to within a distance of 50 feet. Ground squirrels were observed to be fairly numerous on the tundra, and a large colony of hoary marmots was encountered near the head of Frost Creek. The recent track of a single caribou was observed at the edge of a small lake in a tundra basin near the head of Frost Creek. One ptarmigan was flushed at timberline. We traveled an estimated 25 miles on the round trip.

Upon returning to the camp I learned that during the morning Col. Snyder had shot a small bear which entered one of the tents.

The plane flew one load of fuel from Fort Simpson to be used later in flying to be done west from the camp.

August 8 - I set the fish net in the shallow water near the mouth of Frost Creek, and remained in the vicinity of the camp. In walking about one-half mile west of camp, one recent bear scat containing cranberries, and one containing the hair of either moose or caribou, were observed. Mrs. Snyder reported seeing a bull moose at the west end of the lake.

August 9 - We all remained in camp awaiting the return of the aircraft to fly us further up the Nahanni to another lake. I lifted the fish net taking 15 lake trout and 27 grayling. As the aircraft arrived too late to fly that day, we prepared to leave the next day.

August 10 - Col. Snyder and I, with part of the equipment, were flown up the left main fork of the Nahanni above Brintnell Lake. The destination was a small lake about 100 miles up the Nahanni from Brintnell Lake, upon which Col. Snyder was supposed to have landed several years earlier. Most of the Nahanni Valley above Brintnell Lake was observed to carry spruce on the lower slopes, although about one-third of this had been burned over. As we flew further up the valley the spruce became smaller and more scattered. We arrived at the lake indicated on the map by Col. Snyder to find it rather short for the Ballanca take-off, and with a shoal in the middle. After circling this lake several times, the pilot decided not to attempt a landing. We then flew a wide circle along the height of land marking the Yukon-N.W.T. boundary. This is a high rolling plateau carrying tundra vegetation on the knolls and sparse, stunted spruce in the small ravines. Following this we returned to Brintnell Lake. The plane then flew Col. Snyder, Dr. Jennings, and Mr. Griffith on an exploratory trip down the Nahanni to look over the country between the Nahanni and the Flat River. Dr. Jennings, an accurate observer, reported a group of five goats in the rugged mountains south of Virginia Falls.

August 11 - I climbed the slope north of Brintnell Lake, followed Frost Creek to near its head, and climbed the ridge west of the creek. On this ridge I observed a few tracks of both sheep and caribou, made that summer. One ptarmigan on Frost Creek and two golden eagles flying high over the valley were seen. The aircraft flew in a load of fuel from Fort Simpson, and on the return trip took out Mr. Griffith who had twisted a knee badly and wished to return to Calgary.

August 12 - I remained in the vicinity of the camp, sawed firewood, and did other camp shores. Sixteen small lake trout and grayling were taken in the gill net in about 45 minutes fishing at the mouth of Frost Creek.

In the evening two strangers hailed from across the lake, and Dr. Jennings picked them up with the dinghy. They were members of a party of five American university students interested in mountaineering, who were visiting the Brintnell Lake area to climb some of the mountain peaks and to collect data on the geology of the area, the icefield south of Brintnell Lake in particular. This group had been flown to Brintnell lake from Watson Lake, Y.T., by Dalziel Flying Service. The two men who visited our camp were John Bailar and George Yntema, both of Yale University. The three other members of the party, who were camped up the Rapids River at the foot of the main glacier, were Howell Martyn and Dudley Bolyard of Yale, and Harry Nance of the University of Colorado.

August 13 - I remained in the vicinity of the camp, interviewing the mountaineers regarding their observations, and carrying out camp chores.

August 14 - I traveled to the east end of the lake with the collapsible dinghy, taking the two mountaineers to their cache for a supply of provisions.

August 15 - I accompanied the two mountaineers backpacking up the Rapids River about eight miles, to a gravel flood plain at the foot of a glacier, where the other three members of their party were camped.

We followed the right bank of the river, passing through some limited stands of mature white spruce about 12 inches average and 24 inches maximum D.B.H. Some of this timber was dead, apparently from age. Travel was particularly slow and arduous in some places due to windfalls. Several very old abandoned beaver dams were seen in a snye (abandoned channel) of the Rapids River. I observed an adult bear with a yearling or two-year-old on the left side of the river about seven miles up the river from its mouth. They were seen only briefly, running

177

across an opening in the timber, apparently having been alarmed. Although these bears were tan in colour, I was unable to identify them as grizzlies or black bears from the brief glimpse obtained. Deer sign and moose sign were observed frequently en route.

August 16 - I waded across the Rapids River and climbed the slope on the northwest side. Moose and bear sign were observed fairly frequently, and the tracks of two or three caribou were seen.

August 17 - I walked about five miles up the Rapids River from the mountaineers' camp at the foot of the glacier to the head of the river. This river flows through a valley, in some places having worn a small canyon in the limestone and in other places spreading out in braided channels over a gravel flood plain. The valley carries a heavy growth of willows along the river's edge, a band of white spruce adjacent to this, and a band of mixed shrubs between the spruce and the tundra of the higher elevations. The willows showed moderate winter and summer moose browse utilization, and fresh moose sign was abundant. One wolf track was observed on the river beach. A flock of about 15 ptarmigan was flushed. The tracks of three caribou were followed the length of the river above the mountaineers' camp. These followed the river beach most of the way. A few recent beaver cuttings were observed at the river's edge near where the water from the glacier drains into the river.

August 18 - I returned down the Rapids River from the glacier to Snyder's camp. One spruce grouse was observed en route. In the abandoned river channels near the mouth of the river two active beaver colonies were located, and sign of others was seen. Several old dams were found in this vicinity.

On returning to camp I learned that on August 15, Dr. Jennings had shot a solitary bull caribou which swam across the lake from north to south near the camp.

Donald Flook and John Bailer, heading up Brintnell Creek with supplies for exploring the Brintnell Glacier, 1952.

August 19 - I remained in camp. The other members of the party climbed the slope north of the lake to the hanging valley of Frost Creek, where they observed one young bull moose and a herd of 11 caribou, one of which, a mature bull, was collected by Kilgour.

August 20 - I cleaned the skulls of the two caribou taken, and worked with Kilgour and Col. Snyder scraping the skins.

August 21 - Rain. Finished cleaning specimens.

August 22 - Rain. In the afternoon we observed a young bull moose swim half way across the lake from the south side, and turn back to the shore.

August 23 - Rain. I set the fish net in the evening and removed five grayling in about five minutes time.

August 24 - I lifted the fish net, taking 36 fish. The sky cleared in the afternoon.

August 25 - I started to climb up the slope north of the lake and, when about 1,500 feet higher than the lake, observed a bear wade into the lake at the south side and begin to swim across.

I ran down the slope to camp in time to see the bear. Close inspection with binoculars revealed it to be black in color and species. It climbed out of the water at the north side of the lake. I climbed the slope once more and in the upper valley of Frost Creek observed the fresh sign of two or three moose. In the evening the aircraft arrived from Fort Simpson to fly the party to Hay River.

August 26 - The aircraft left for Hay River with Col. and Mrs. Snyder, their nephew, and Dr. Jennings. Kilgour and I were to be flown out with the remainder of the equipment as soon as the plane could return.

August 27 - It rained all day. In the evening we observed a single grey wolf feeding on the caribou entrails left on the beach across the lake. Kilgour and I each fired a shot at the animal but missed it.

August 28 - It had snowed during the night on the mountains down to about 3,500 feet elevation. Two mallard ducks were observed on the lake, and an osprey was seen to catch a fish. In the afternoon while I was walking down the lakeshore about one-half mile from camp, Kilgour observed at the camp an adult bear showing the same structural characteristics as the black bear, and the brown and tan coloration of the bear killed by Snyder (described later).

August 29 -The weather was clear, and the aircraft arrived from Fort Simpson to pick up Kilgour and me. On his trip in, the pilot picked up three prospectors at Virginia Falls and flew them to Brintnell Lake where they plan to do more prospecting. These men were Ollie Rollog and Slim Raider, two old timers with considerable experience in the country, and David Aoncia, a younger man. They are all from Whitehorse and early in July were flown by Dalziel Airways to Brintnell lake from whence they walked and paddled an improvised canoe to Virginia Falls.

We took off from Brintnell Lake at 1:15 p.m. and, flying by way of the South Nahanni River, arrived at Fort Simpson about 3:30

p.m. After a brief stop, the plane with Kilgour returned to Hay River.

Wildlife Observations

Mammals

BLACK BEAR - *Euarctos* sp. Well-worn trails and frequent scats and claw marks indicated the presence of a fair population of bears, mostly of the black species, in the Brintnell Lake valley, on adjacent slopes, and along the water courses feeding the lake. Black bears were observed by members of the Snyder expedition on five different occasions within a two-mile radius of camp, and these were four and possibly five different bears. Three of the observations were of bears of a typical black color. An adult and juvenile observed in the immediate vicinity of camp had dark brown pelage over all the body, with a long, light tan mane or roach on the shoulders. The juvenile was shot by Col. Snyder when it entered one of the tents. As I was not in the camp at the time, it was killed and butchered without measurements being obtained. After examining the pelt, I concluded that the odd coloration could be explained as due to the moult not having been completed. The long mane was the only part of the old hair remaining and was faded in contrast to the new dark hair over the rest of the body. The skin is in the possession of Col. Snyder. I forwarded the skull to Mr. Austin Cameron of the National Museum for identification and retention by the museum. He identified it tentatively as *Euarctos americanus* (American Black Bear), but as there was a possibility that it might be referred to *Euarctos hunteri* (Big Northwestern Black Bear), he advised that further cleaning and measuring of the skull would be necessary before definite identification could be made.

GRIZZLY BEAR - *Ursus* sp. Although claw marks on trees and elsewhere probably made by grizzly bears were observed, no clear tracks or sight observations were made which can be definitely attributed to bears of this genus. On August 15, the writer caught a short glimpse of an adult and a juvenile bear,

181

both reddish tan in color, running across a small clearing about seven miles up the Rapids River from its mouth. It is possible that they were grizzlies although they might have been black bears. Ollie Rollog, one of the prospectors interviewed at Brintnell Lake, reported seeing a grizzly on the Nahanni a few miles east of Brintnell Lake in July.

TIMBER WOLF - *Canus lupus occidentalis* (Richardson). One wolf track was observed by the writer on August 17, on a sand bar in the Rapids River about ten miles up the river from its mouth. On August 27 one wolf feeding on caribou entrails was observed on the south shore of the lake.

ALASKA MARTEN - *Martes Americana actuosa* (Osgood). The Yale mountaineering party reported observing a marten at their cache on the east end of the lake.

WOLVERINE - *Gulo luscus luscus* (Linnaeus). The fresh track of a wolverine was reported by Kilgour, a reliable observer, on the slope southeast of Brintnell Lake on August 6.

COLLARED PIKA - *Ochotona collaris* (Nelson). The Yale mountaineering party reported observing pika on some of the higher mountains in the area.

MACKENZIE VARYING HARE - *Lepus americanus macfarlani* Merriam. The fecal pellets of hare were observed sparsely scattered in the timbered areas about the lake.

ROCKY MOUNTAIN HOARY MARMOT - *Marmota caligata oxytoma* Hollister. A large colony of marmots was observed near the head of Frost Creek. Mr. Cameron [curator of mammals - eds] identified one specimen collected there and forwarded it to the National Museum.

YUKON GROUND SQUIRREL - *Citellus plesius plesius* (Osgood). Ground squirrels were observed to be fairly abundant on the tundra, especially on Frost Creek.

George Yntema and John Bailar at Snyder's camp at the mouth of Frost Creek, 13 August 1952. Photo Donald Flook.

YUKON CHIPMUNK - *Eutamius minimus caniceps* (Osgood). Several chipmunks were observed along the banks of the Rapids River.

MACKENZIE RED SQUIRREL - *Tamiasciurus hudsonicus preblei* Howell. Red squirrels were observed to be numerous throughout the timbered area about Brintnell Lake. One specimen was sent to the National Museum and identified by Mr. Cameron.

CANADA BEAVER - *Castor canadensis canadensis* Kuhl. Three active beaver colonies were located on the snyes on the delta of the Rapids River. Several very old dams, some probably thirty years old, were found in the same locality. Recent cuttings were found on the Rapids River near timberline where the glacier water drains into the river. One of the Yale mountaineers [Howell Martyn - eds] reported that in rafting down about 75 miles of the Nahanni above Brintnell Lake, in early July, he observed about 100 beaver.

ALASKA PORCUPINE - *Erethizon dorsatum myops* Merriam. One of the members of the Yale mountaineering party gave the writer a handful of wolf hair matted with porcupine quills. He had found this clinging to a shrub near the west end of the lake.

WESTERN MOOSE - *Alces americana andersoni* Peterson. Moose sign, recent and from the previous winter, was observed quite frequently from the timbered valley floor around the lake to the willow ravines of the high elevations. Moose were observed by the writer on two occasions. On August 6 Kilgour and I observed a medium-sized bull, which was aged, judging from its swayed back. It was lying on an isolated snow bank in a ravine high above timberline when first observed. We stalked it to within a distance of 50 feet. When it saw us it stood up, walked a few steps, and stopped to look us over, before trotting leisurely down the ravine. I doubt from its behaviour that this moose had any previous contact with man. One bull was observed in this same vicinity by Kilgour on August 19. On August 22 a young bull was observed to enter the water of the lake on the opposite shore from the camp, and about 1 1/2 miles east. It swam about one-half way across the lake (about 3/4 mile wide) and after hesitating twice, returned to the point from whence it had set out. A bull moose was observed by Mrs. Snyder near the lake on another occasion. Although the tracks of adults with calves were observed on several occasions, no cow or calf moose were actually observed. Judging from the frequency of pellet groups and the intensity of browse utilization, the greatest concentrations of moose are found in the areas along the water courses. Willows, *Salix* spp., are the key browse species, and dwarf birch, *Betula glandulosa* is of secondary importance. On the basis of the past winter's utilization of the willow browse along the creeks, the forage would carry a larger moose population than now exists in the Brintnell lake area. The two prospectors interviewed at Brintnell Lake who have done considerable prospecting in this area in past years, and who this year traveled from Brintnell Lake to Virginia Falls on foot and by canoe, reported that they observed moose as well as sheep to be fewer in numbers this season than in previous years. They said that wolves were more numerous in the area in past years when big game was more abundant.

It seems quite possible that one or more seasons of extremely heavy snowfall may have resulted in severe winter mortality from secondary causes. It is also possible that winters of extremely heavy snowfall may have forced the moose to follow the valley of the South Nahanni River down to lower elevations where conditions were more favorable. I observed evidence of snow slides of recent years on slopes where one would not expect these to occur under conditions of moderate snowfall.

As this area is very isolated and inaccessible, and as there have been no NWT trappers in the area for many years, it is believed that the moose population of the area has not been greatly influenced by hunting in recent years.

CARIBOU (probably Osborne) - *Rangifer arcticus osborni* Allen. Tracks of a few caribou were observed by the writer in the upper valley of Frost Creek above timberline, and also along the upper portions of the Rapids River. The Yale mountaineers reported seeing small groups of caribou in several locations on the high plateaus south of Brintnell Lake. One solitary adult bull was shot by Dr. Jennings on August 15, when it swam across the lake in front of the camp. I estimated the weight of this specimen at 400 pounds. The pelage was almost uniformly medium brown in color. The antlers, which had not yet fully developed their palmations, were in velvet of a mousy color. Col. Snyder has, I understand, forwarded the skull and skin of this specimen to the national Museum. On August 19 a second bull caribou was taken by Kilgour in the upper valley of Frost Creek. The skull and skin of this specimen also were forwarded to the National Museum by Col Snyder. Kilgour, who accompanied Col. Snyder and the other members of the party on this occasion, reported that they encountered a group of eleven caribou which he classified as 2 bulls, 8 cows or yearling bulls, and 1 calf. I estimated the weight of this specimen at 300 pounds. It was somewhat smaller, and the pelage and antler velvet darker than those of the first specimen taken. Some Indians and prospectors have reported that there are two kinds of caribou in the Mackenzie Mountains: one a non-migratory woodland type, probably *Rangifer caribou sylvestris* (Richardson), and the other a migratory type, probably *Rangifer arcticus osborni* Allen. However, the difference between the two specimens taken is no greater in degree than the variation which I have observed among the barren ground caribou near Fort Rae, and I suspect that the two specimens are of the same subspecies, although I have not learned the National Museum identification.

DALL'S SHEEP - *Ovis dalli dalli* (Nelson). A few recent tracks of sheep were observed by the writer on the shores of the small lake high above timberline at the head of Frost Creek. The tracks of two or three sheep were also observed on the shore of Brintnell lake at the mouth of Frost Creek. The Yale mountaineers also saw tracks which they believe to be those of sheep. No sheep were actually observed by either the Snyder expedition or the Yale mountaineers. This would seem to indicate a low population level of the species in this area, as large expanses of favorable sheep habitat were observed both north and south of the lake.

COLUMBIAN MOUNTAIN GOAT - *Oreamnos americanus columbiae* Hollister. A handful of silky hair was shown to the writer by one of the Yale mountaineering group who had found it clinging to a rock on a high mountain west of Brintnell lake. This was definitely the hair of a mountain goat. Dr. Jennings, who is a reliable observer, reported seeing a group of five goats in the rugged mountains south of Virginia Falls, in flying over that area on August 10.

Birds casually observed about Brintnell Lake were as follows:

MALLARD DUCK - Two females were observed frequently near the camp, and nine ducks and drakes were seen on the east end of the lake, August 26.

AMERICAN GOLDEN-EYE - One female observed at the east end of the lake on August 5.

SCAUP - (Lesser or Greater?) - Eight were observed near the east end of the lake on August 26.

SHARP-SHINNED HAWK - one was observed a short distance below timberline on Frost Creek on August 5.

GOLDEN EAGLE - The shrill cry of a golden eagle was heard from the camp on August 5, and on August 11 two golden eagles were observed flying over the high slopes along Frost Creek.

PTARMIGAN (probably of the willow species) - One ptarmigan was observed on each of the three occasions I ascended Frost Creek. A flock of about 15 were observed on August 17, on the upper part of the Rapids River. As on each occasion these were seen in the willow bottoms along a watercourse, they were probably of the willow species.

SPOTTED SANDPIPER - These were frequently observed along the lake shore.

CANADA JAY - Several of these birds could be seen about the camp at all times.

SLATE-COLOURED JUNCO - A small flock of these was observed near the lake shore on August 6.

From "Marten in the Central Mackenzie Region/Season 1952-53," by Donald R. Flook

There are two good marten producing areas in that portion of the Liard District which has been registered in trapping areas. The first area lies around Trout Lake and is a fairly high, well drained plateau. Although part of this country was burned over in the large fire of 1943 - 44, there remain large tracts of mature green timber which produce a large number of marten with high quality pelts. Mr. Dick Turner says that he believes he could harvest annually 35 marten from his registered trapping area which lies on the east side of Trout Lake. Last year, all the Indian trappers in the Trout Lake group area, including the women, filled their marten permits, and I was informed at Fort Liard that this season they had filled their permits before Christmas.

The other good marten producing section of registered territory in the Liard District, lies between the Liard River and the Yukon boundary. This is mountainous country, and the timbered slopes produce large numbers of marten. The Indians holding registered trapping areas in this section filled their quotas last season.

There also lies in the Liard District a large tract of open territory (not registered). This includes all the watershed of the South Nahanni River above Lafferty Creek. This area is reputed to have produced large catches of marten of high quality dark pelts in earlier years. There were a few Indian trappers from Fort Simpson and Fort Liard, as well as a few white trappers, operating in the area some 15 years ago. I gather that it was largely as a result of the undesirable trapping practices of some of these white trappers that the restrictions to trapping in the Mackenzie Mountains were instituted. These restrictions were: (1) the establishment of the Mackenzie Mountains Native Game Preserve; (2) a bag limit on marten; (3) prohibiting a trapper from flying into the Preserve. However, these regulations created to protect the interests of the Indian trappers, combined with poor fur market conditions, have made it impossible for the NWT Indian trappers to utilize this remote area economically. There are rumours that poachers from the Yukon operated in the Flat River country within the past five years.

Marten Survey -- South Nahanni Watershed

In order to study the conditions of the upper Nahanni region with regard to the abundance of marten and condition of the area as marten habitat, a survey was conducted on March 23 to 26. An Associated Airways Beaver aircraft, piloted by R. Rutherford was chartered. I was accompanied by Chief Warden W. Day and Gus Kraus, white trapper from the mouth of the South Nahanni, who acted as guide. Kraus has prospected and trapped in the Nahanni and is very familiar with the country.

March 23 - We encountered fog in the Flat and it was due to Kraus' knowledge of the lay of the land that we were able to land on Seaplane Lake at 5:10 p.m. Here we located and camped in an old cabin built by Kraus when prospecting many years ago. Although he had not been there since 1945, there were signs that the cabin had been used for long periods at several different times in recent years. During the evening, Day and I snowshoed about 1 1/2 miles northwest from the lake, up a timbered slope, through mature stands of white spruce, black spruce and jack pine. We observed a few snowshoe hare tracks and a few red squirrel tracks, but no marten tracks. Two or three inches of snow fell during the night.

March 24 - Temperature 25 degrees F, sky overcast, light snowfall during early morning. The weather was unsuitable for flying all day which was to our advantage as this made it possible for us to spend the entire day exploring the area without any charge for holding the aircraft. In the morning Kraus and I snowshoed three miles northwest from the lake and completed a circle of about seven miles, returning to the cabin. We

Donald Flook and Gus Kraus, with canoe and skiff lashed together, traveling up the lower South Nahanni.

observed four old moose tracks, five old lynx tracks, two old wolf tracks, 1 spruce grouse, 1 snowshoe hare, but no sign of marten. I picked up two rusted steel traps, a No. 1 1/2 and a No. 4, hanging on a tree. Day walked south from camp for about two hours and reported no marten sign.

During the afternoon, Gus and I snowshoed to a cabin across the Flat River, and returned, a round trip of about nine miles. This cabin which belongs to Albert Faille, a prospector, had not apparently been used recently and was in decaying condition. We observed five old moose tracks on the Flat River, and also an otter track which ended at a patch of open water in the river. On the return trip, the sky partially cleared for a short time, and the red squirrels became active. One was collected. No marten tracks were observed on this trip.

The area about Seaplane Lake is well covered with mature timber: white spruce, black spruce, canoe birch, jackpine, black poplar, and white poplar. The heaviest timber observed was on the banks of the Flat River where there are white spruce, 24 inches D.B.H.

<u>March 25</u> - Temperature 25 degrees F, partly cloudy. In the morning we flew from Seaplane Lake southwestward and landed at McMillan Lake some 20 miles distant. In the vicinity of this lake there are large tracts of timber: white spruce, black spruce, and jackpine, averaging about 6 inches D.B.H. There is a large burn about 15 years old, northwest of the lake.

Kraus and I snowshoed about four miles southwest from the lake, travelling partly on the valley bottom, partly on the slopes. We passed a cabin which Kraus built about 15 years ago. It is in a poor state of repair and showed no sign of recent occupation. We observed the tracks of a group of about six caribou on the lake ice, and a few old moose tracks, a few squirrel tracks, and four weasel tracks in the timber. However, we saw no sign of marten and no sign of snowshoe hare. While we were making this reconnaisance, Day snowshoed up the slope due south of the lake and reported no sign of marten.

We then took off from McMillan Lake and flew down the Flat River as far as Irvine Creek; thence up Irvine Creek over a pass into the valley of the South Nahanni itself, above Virginia Falls. We proceeded up the Nahanni, intending to land either on the river ice or on one of the unmapped lakes near the river. However, we observed no suitable place for a landing until we reached Brintnell Lake where we landed. On this flight we observed fresh tracks of small bands of caribou from McMillan lake to the Flat River, and along Irvine Creek, where we observed one caribou on a lake. Along the South Nahanni River from Irvine Creek to Glacier Lake, we observed tracks of large numbers of caribou mostly on and around abandoned river channels and in areas which from the air appeared to be meadows of grass-like plants. We were flying at high altitude and were not able to see any of the caribou although the tracks would indicate the presence of a large herd.

At Brintnell Lake, Kraus and I showshoed a circle of about five miles on the timbered slope north of the lake. In this route we observed 32 marten tracks crossing our trail. These were dis-

tributed from the lake shore to the highest point to which we climbed, about 500 feet above the lake. Nine tracks were fresh and 23 were covered with light snow fallen probably during the previous night. We observed about 40 red squirrel tracks on the same route, and no sign of snowshoe hare. We observed the tracks of six caribou that moved up the slope, feeding occasionally on *Cladonia*, and also the track of an otter on the lake.
. . .

Trappers who have trapped marten in the Mackenzie Mountains have reported that marten frequent the forested areas of the slopes adjacent to timber-line, through the winter until March, when they begin to travel extensively and can be trapped on the lower slopes and valley bottoms. It is reported that they can be trapped as long as snow remains.

I believe that, had there been marten in the areas explored in the Flat River, i.e. Seaplane Lake and McMillan Lake, some tracks would have been observed. Trappers interviewed, who operated in the South Nahanni in earlier years, reported that Seaplane Lake and McMillan Lake were both areas in which large numbers of marten were trapped in early years. The upper Flat River area is easily accessible from the Yukon, Seaplane Lake being only 10 miles from the boundary and McMillan Lake about 22 miles. It is reported that a route traveled by Yukon trappers to enter the Northwest Territories is from Francis Lake, YT, to the headwaters of the Flat River and Caribou River. Poachers from the Yukon were rumored to be operating in that area four years ago, and it is possible that they so depleted the marten that they discontinued trapping.

Brintnell Lake is separated from the nearest point on the Yukon boundary by some 20 miles of very rugged terrain. The easiest land route from the Yukon is via the Nahanni Valley which is a long route. In my travel last summer in the vicinity of Brintnell Lake I observed no indication of trapping activity. The great frequency of marten tracks in the area covered at Brintnell Lake is indicative of a good marten population. As there are large tracts of similar forest cover suitable for marten along the Nahanni Valley both above and below Brintnell Lake, and as this country has not been trapped for many years, it very probably carries a large population of marten . . .

"Checklist" from <u>Birds of Nahanni National Park</u> by George W. Scotter, Ludwig N. Carbyn, Wayne P. Neily and J. David Henry. 1985. Special publication No. 15 of the Saskatchewan Natural History Society.

[Park visitors are invited to sent bird sightings to the Superintent of Nahanni National Park. Most of the sightings listed in this book are based on sightings by Henry at Deadmen Valley and the confluence of the Flat and South Nahanni rivers. Other sightings are by Scotter, Carbyn, and Neily in these and other areas. R.M. Patterson's <u>Beaver</u> articles provided some sightings, and Mickey Kraus (Gus Kraus's son) sent in sightings from Kraus Hotsprings. The CWS officers regarded him as a very good birder. Visitors to the park also contributed. Contributions from Glacier Lake would be welcomed as only Flook and Scotter have provided formal sightings from that area - eds.]

Bird names and order follow the 6th edition of <u>the American Ornithologists' Union Check-list of North American Birds</u> (1983)

The letters preceding each species name are in the order of:
<u>Abundance</u> (C: common; U: uncommon; R: rare; H: hypothetical)
<u>Seasonal Status</u> (M: migrant; S: summer; W: winter; P: permanent; U: unknown)
<u>Breeding Status</u> (1: proven; 2: probable; 3: possible)

US3 Red-throated Loon
US3 Arctic Loon
CS1 Common Loon
HS- Yellow-Billed Loon
RS3 Pied-Billed Loon
US1 Horned Grebe
CS1 Red-Necked Grebe
RS1 Trumpeter Swan
HM- Greater White-Fronted Goose
CM3 Canada Goose
CS1 Greened-Winged Teal
CS1 Mallard
US3 Northern Pintail

US3 Blue-Winged Teal
RS3 Northern Shoveler
HS1 Gadwall
US1 American Wigeon
RS3 Ring-Necked Duck
HM-Greater Scaup
CS1 Lesser Scaup
UM- Oldsquaw
CS2 Surfscoter
CS3 White-Winged Scoter
CS1 Common Goldeneye
RS1 Barrow's Goldeneye
CS1 Bufflehead
US3 Common Merganser
US3 Red-Breasted Merganser
RS3 Osprey
US1 Bald Eagle
US1 Northern Harrier
US1 Sharp-Shinned Hawk
RS3 Northern Goshawk
RS- Swainson's Hawk
US2 Red-Tailed Hawk
US1 Golden Eagle
CS1 American Kestrel
RS2 Merlin
RS2 Peregrine Falcon
RS- Gyrfalcon
CP1 Spruce Grouse
UP3 Blue Grouse
HP- Willow Ptarmigan
UP3 Rock Ptarmigan
UP2 White-Tailed Ptarmigan
CP1 Ruffed Grouse
RP- Sharp-Tailed Grouse
US1 Sora
US3 American Coot
RM-Sandhill Crane

RS2 Lesser Golden-Plover
CM- Semipalmated Plover
RM- Killdeer
UM-Greater Yellowlegs
CS1 Lesser Yellowlegs
US2 Solitary Sandpiper
RS3 Wandering Tattler
CS1 Spotted Sandpiper
US1 Upland Sandpiper
Cm- Semipalmated Sandpiper
HM- Western Sandpiper
US1 Least Sandpiper
RM- White-Rumped Sandpiper
RM- Baird's Sandpiper
HM- Stilt Sandpiper
CS1 Common Snipe
CM- Red-Necked Phalarope
CS2 Bonaparte's Gull
CS2 Mew Gull
US3 Herring Gull
CS1 Arctic Tern
RS2 Black Tern
UP2 Great Horned Owl
HU- Northern Hawk-Owl
HU- Barred Owl
HP- Great Gray Owl
CS1 Common Nighthawk
HU- Hummingbird
CS3 Belted Kingfisher
CS1 Yellow-Bellied Sapsucker
US3 Downy Woodpecker
UP1 Hairy Woodpecker
CP1 Three-Toed Woodpecker
RP3 Black-Backed Woodpecker
CS1 Northern Flicker
RS3 Pileated Woodpecker
US3 Olive-Sided Flycatcher

US2 Western Wood-Pewee
RM- Yellow-Bellied Flycatcher
US3 Alder Flycatcher
US2 Least Flycatcher
US2 Hammond's Flycatcher
RS 2 Eastern Phoebe
US3 Eastern Kingbird
CS2 Horned Lark
CS1 Tree Swallow
CS1 Violet-Green Swallow
CS1 Bank Swallow
CS2 Cliff Swallow
CP2 Gray Jay
HS- Clark's Nutcracker
HM- American Crow
CP1 Common Raven
CP3 Black-Capped Chickadee
CP1 Boreal Chickadee
RS3 Red-Breasted Nuthatch
RP3 American Dipper
RS- Golden-Crowned Kinglet
US3 Ruby-Crowned Kinglet
HM- Mountain Bluebird
CS3 Townsend's Solitaire
CS1 Gray-Cheeked Thrush
CS1 Swainson's Thrush
CS1 Hermit Thrush
CS1 American Robin
CS1 Varied Thrush
CS1 Water Pipit
CS1 Bohemian Waxwing
RS3 Northern Shrike
RS1 European Starling
US1 Warbling Vireo
RS- Philadelphia Vireo
US1 Red-Eyed Vireo
CS1 Tennessee Warbler

CS1 Yellow Warbler
US3 Magnolia Warbler
CS1 Yellow-Rumped Warbler
RS- Black-Throated Green Warbler
RS3 Palm Warbler
RS2 Bay-Breasted Warbler
US3 Blackpoll Warbler
US3 Black-and-White Warbler
RS3 American Redstart
US2 Ovenbird
US3 Northern Waterthrush
US3 Mourning Warbler
US3 Common Yellowthroat
UM- Wilson's Warbler
US3 Western Tanager
RS- Rose-Breasted Grosbeak
CS2 American Tree Sparrow
CS1 Chipping Sparrow
US3 Clay-Colored Sparrow
RS3 Vesper Sparrow
US1 Savannah Sparrow
US3 Fox Sparrow
US3 Song Sparrow
CS1 Lincoln's Sparrow
US1 Swamp Sparrow
CS1 White-Throated Sparrow
US1 Golden-Crowned Sparrow
CS1 White-Crowned Sparrow
CS1 Dark-Eyed Junco
CM- Lapland Longspur
RS- Smith's Longspur
RM- Snow Bunting
CS2 Red-Winged Blackbird
US3 Rusty Blackbird
US2 Brown-Headed Cowbird
US3 Rosy Finch
RP3 Pine Grosbeak

Gus and Mary Kraus with Lucy Donta (swatting a mosquito) at the Kraus cabin, May 1953. Photo: Donald Flook.

RS2 Purple Finch
CS1 White-Winged Crossbill
UP3 Common Redpoll
CW- Hoary Redpoll
CS3 Pine Siskin
RU- Evening Grosbeak

Raymond Patterson

I meant to ask you about Harry Snyder. You gave me an address for his wife, his second wife, and I have never gotten to writing her.

I wonder how she is. I've usually had a Christmas card from her and I don't remember getting one this winter, but I sent one down to Tucson. That's where I last heard of her.

When Harry Snyder's home up in the Red Deer valley burned, did he lose all his photographs and records and everything of the Nahanni or did any of them ever survive?

I don't think they all perished by any means. But he moved what survived, whatever that was, the fire, and I rather think he made quite a name for himself in Tucson talking about the country and lecturing about the country. He had a wonderful way of putting things over. I mean whether he was certain about a thing or not there'd be no "I think" about it. He would say absolutely what it was. . . It would seem to squelch all questioning. I rather think he left a good deal of his stuff to some historical society in Tucson. Whether he left that Arctic stuff . . . I don't know who he would leave it to. They may have liked it knowing him, and he being a resident.

Was he the kind of man that would have kept a diary?

No, I wouldn't have thought so, except possibly on a trip. Any more than I would. I mean I've kept diaries on trips.

The reason I ask is I'm trying to track down some sort of an account of a number of his expeditions and so far I haven't been very successful at it.

The numbers of his expeditions. I don't know how many times he got into that country. He had a passion for that Glacier Lake country and I should've thought it was the last place to go on a hunting trip by the look of it.

Yes. I think the last time was 1952 that he went in and there was a Colonel A. J. Sandy McNab was along. Does that name ring any bells?

Oh yes. That was one that associated with some of his trips. Is McNab still around do you know? I've no idea. Was he an official of the American Natural Museum of Natural History?

No, no. I've tried to trace the museum people and haven't been successful.

Have you read his African books?

No I haven't.

Do you have that . . .

Snyder's Book of Big-Game Hunting, it's called.

That was the main book. I don't know whether he wrote any other actual books.

I've also tried to find Harry Lambart who was the surveyor on one of his early expeditions at Glacier lake but I can't find any record of him. There's a doctor Jennings that was in Calgary but I believe he'd died now.

He died now. I knew him very well and liked him. Then there was E. J. Johnson, a very old man now. Great friend of the Colonel's. He lives in Scarsdale, New York. He was chief counsel to the Standard Oil of New Jersey . . . .

Would there be anybody else that you could think of offhand that might have information on his expeditions?

Ed Johnson is the only one I can think of now. Harry James, maybe. . . .

Bill Clark

[Clark questioned about Lambart, Goodwin, and the dates of Snyder's expeditions. Clark has no ideas on these questions -eds.]

Snyder took a lot of photographs and did a lot of surveying and I can't find the records of his material at all.

I'll tell you. He was in with George Roberts, a friend of mine. In fact, he climbed to the top of Cathedral Mountain and put in a cairn, with Lambart.

Is George Roberts still around?

Trouble is he died about I think it was a year-and-a-half ago, out in B.C. And his wife is still alive, but . . .

Was George Roberts . . . the type that would've taken any photographs?

He was relaying for Snyder's outfit . . . . Snyder was taking in a lot of, quite a few of his friends, and George was relaying from the mouth of the Nahanni, up to the falls, foot of the falls, and then took his friends and stuff over the portage there. The plane would come and pick them up there and take them into Glacier Lake.

Snyder published an article, Lambart published one, George Goodwin published a couple. But there's a lot of little details would be interesting to know and . . . photographs which would be nice to have.

Well I know George did take pictures. By Jove, I don't know where they would be. I don't know whether his wife, his widow, that'd be pretty well easy to check up alright, because she had a family before marriage and her son . . . She was Mrs. Jones, and her son is the Imperial agent at Inuvik, Dave Jones. He would know.

Gus Kraus

What is the first year you recall Harry Snyder coming into the country.

Snyder came in '35 . . . Went to Glacier Lake, always to Glacier Lake, and after he got to Glacier Lake then he went to Dal Lake and at Dal Lake he was going to put a . . . build a cabin in there. They flew in a bunch of hardwood flooring. He was going to make a resort for him and his cronies, because he had a hunting lodge at Dorothy Lake.

Where's that?

B.C.

Oh, yeh.

Now he was putting this one in at Dal Lake. All for the sheep, because, remember I told you, I seen one of his pictures with three hundred sheep in one bunch . . . There's trout in the lake too and he was going to build there. So then every year, the only way he could come in was by asking for, getting permit for research. The last time, he was allowed to come in to kill five sheep because he was making research on where they get their black hair in the sheep's tail. . . . So he got quite a few. Black hair on dall sheep even, not only in the tail, but in the whole body . . . real jet black hair. That was his excuse to get the permits, to kill five more sheep. Then he wanted to prove he could kill a grizzly with one shot. So, they flew in a canoe in there and put a nice big Morris chair in it. He paddled it up and down watching that side-hill. You've been to . . . you know Glacier Lake . . . a side-hill. They figured you could see a grizzly coming there, you're going to knock him over in one shot. That was the last. From there on, no more Harry Snyder came. Well, then he got sick and he went back to Calgary. He's supposed to have a million dollar mansion somewheres back in Calgary there with all his trophies in it.

He did.

You know he had the record on the elephant tusk . . twelve foot?
Yeh. That's sure a big one. It all burnt . . . .

Did you ever run into Snyder, ever meet him?

Once, yeh.

What year was that?

That was in '37. No, '36. . . . He's a nice guy, nice man to talk
to, awful interested in wildlife, everything, no matter if it was
plants or anything. But he was really a hunter. He's not a con-
servationist because he liked to kill.

My records seem to indicate '37.

Could be.

*Yeh. That was the year he had his really big expedition into the
country I think.*

Yeh, he at that time had Oldman in and McBrady, two govern-
ment guys. One was a mammalogist . . . .

Goodwin.

Yeh, an awkward one. The other one was a plant life
[researcher] taking all the plants . . . . They had whole trunks
full of . . . lynx and stuff, skinned mice, name it, the marmots
and everything. . . . That's the time he wanted to get that sheep
. . . . It was called Cathedral Range, from the head of the
Nahanni to the Flat, that big high range.

That's what you people knew it as?

Cathedral Range, yeh. He wanted to get that changed to Snyder
Range. So, they told me they spent forty thousand dollars in
exploration, and turn all the information in to the government,
they'll call it Snyder range. Well they did it, but I only seen one
map that ever it mentioned Snyder Range.

OBITUARIES

Hugh Miller Raup

From "A Tribute to Hugh Miller Raup, 1901-1995, by William J. Cody. Canadian Field Naturalist 112 (1998): 557-564.

Hugh Raup was born 4 February 1901 in Springfield, Ohio, the son of Gustavus and Fannie Raup. He died at Sister Bay, Wisconsin, 10 August 1995. His early education was in public schools and Wittenburgh College at Springfield. He and Lucy Gibson were married 20 June 1925 and were the parents of two sons, Karl and David. The following Memorial Minute for the Faculty of Arts and Sciences of Harvard University dated 8 April 1997 was composed by David R. Foster, Barry Tomlinson, Peter Ashton and Rolla Tryon:

"Hugh Miller Raup was among the last of Harvard's great field naturalists - a botanist, ecologist and geographer who vigorously applied his immense experience in tropical, temperate and arctic landscapes to landmark studies in natural history and natural resource management . . . .

"Upon graduation [from Wittenberg College, 1923] he was appointed as Instructor in Biology and, following receipt of his A.M. degree in 1925 and Ph.D. in 1928 from the University of Pittsburgh, promoted to Assistant Professor at Wittenberg, where he taught until his departure to Harvard in 1932.

"At Harvard, Hugh Raup was associated with four botanical institutions: the Arnold Arboretum . . . the Black Rock Forest . . . the Department of Botany . . . . and the Harvard Forest where he was Director from 1946 to 1967. . . . Subsequently Hugh and Lucy Raup lived for more than 20 years on the Common in Petersham, Massachusetts where Hugh maintained vigorous correspondence with colleagues and challenged emerging scientific minds with his frequent, lengthy letters. In their last years Hugh and Lucy moved to Wisconsin to be near their son Dave. Hugh was predeceased by his elder son Karl.

"Hugh's training in biology and geography and desire to synthesize geological and evolutionary processes in his understanding of natural ecosystems, generated unique contributions to the fields of plant geography, ecology, forestry and natural resources. Beginning with his doctoral research on the vegetation and floristics of the Athabaska-Great Slave Lake Region of Northwestern Canada, Hugh commenced a life-long pursuit documenting the plants and environment of the far north. During subsequent years collaborating with the Canadian National Museum, these studies led Hugh, his family and many colleagues from the boreal forests of Alaska, through subarctic Canada, to the high Arctic of Mesters Veg in northeastern Greenland. Around campfires in the glow of northern summer evenings Hugh and Lucy would undertake the meticulous documentation of field collections that form the basis of all biogeographical study. These summer-long excursions produced a stream of publications . . . .

"Through the course of his career, Hugh's interests broadened beyond plant biology to embrace such topics as Indian archaeology, the role of frost action, lake-level change and winter injury in northern ecosystems, and the influence of natural disturbance and historical land use on forests in Cuba, Honduras, and New England.

"Hugh's personal charm, his delightful habit of challenging new as well as established ideas, and his insights drawn from diverse ecosystems made him an exceptional mentor, colleague and friend . . . . With a tap and fuss at his pipe Hugh always mused carefully over one's remarks and reciprocated with thoughtful and provocative comments."

Hugh's Canadian studies were mainly in the northwest. His work in the Athabaska-Great Slave Lake, Wood Buffalo National park and the Peace and Upper Liard River regions began in 1926 and continued through the summers of 1927, 1928, 1929, 1930, 1932 and 1935. This was the pre-air travel time when movement throughout the area was by steamboat, motor tug, canoe or skiff, pack-horse, wagon or buckboard and by back packing. This meant that food, tents, extra clothing, blankets, plant presses and other equipment had to be portaged through sunshine, wind, rain, mosquitoes and black flies. On many of the excursions Hugh was accompanied by his wife Lucy, who had a particular interest in mosses and lichens. In the lake Athabasca region, at least, the Raups traveled by freighter canoe with their two young children, David and Karl. In addition to collecting lichens and mosses, Lucy looked after the two boys, and was camp cook. Based on about 20 years of field camping, mostly in connection with Hugh's research, Lucy published Camper's Cookbook (Tuttle, 1967). . . .

In 1939 Hugh, again accompanied by his wife Lucy, together with his graduate student James (Jim) H. Soper, extended his work northward into the District of Mackenzie in the vicinities of Fort Simpson . . . and Glacier Lake in the Mackenzie Mountains. This work resulted in the publication of The Botany of Southwestern Mackenzie (1947).

These publications were not just annotated lists of species . . . but included information on earlier explorers, geology and physiography . . . Hugh participated in expeditions to the Alaska Military Highway in 1943 and 1944. Publications did not list the species collected adjacent to the new highway, but described with interesting detail the various vegetation types through which it passed from prairie, wetlands and forests to alpine. . . .

Fred Lambart

"H.F.J. Lambart (1880 - 1946)" Canadian Alpine Journal XXIX. 2 (June 1946): 283-285

Those who had the privilege of friendship with Fred Lambart realize the extent of his enthusiasm for the alpine areas of Canada. Coupled with a keen appreciation of their beauty and recreational value there was also understanding of the opportunity for scientific research.

As a contemporary of the Canadian Alpine Club's first president in the development of photo-topography and later aerial photography for mapping purposes, he made a substantial contribution in topographical surveys, undertaken by the Dominion Government under whose auspices he worked from 1905 until his retirement in 1933, a period which included seven years in charge of the Yukon-Alaska Boundary demarcation.

In connection with his professional work, and as a member of the Club he made many notable ascents including that of Mt. Robson, and was also an outstanding member of the joint Canadian-United States party which did such valuable work in exploration and mountaineering in the Mt. St. Elias Range, including the only ascent of Mt. Logan, the highest mountain in Canadian territory.

His later years made heavy demands upon the courage and confidence which had marked his career, as despite a magnificent physique his demise was preceded by a lengthy illness, in addition to which during the war he lost his two sons, Flying Officer F.A.H. Lambart, R.A.F., and Capt. E.H.W. Lambart, R.C.A.

Surviving are two daughters, Miss Hyacinthe Lambart of the British Aviation Company and Miss Evelyn Lambart of the National Film Board, and a sister Miss Caroline Lambart at home.

Mr. Lambart was a fellow of the Royal Geographic Society and a member of many kindred organizations connected with his profession.

Harry Snyder

"Colonel Harry Snyder Dies in Arizona," Calgary Herald (30 March 1972): 14

Harry M. Snyder, a prominent businessman and Calgary resident from 1955 to 1966, died in Arizona this week.

Mr. Snyder was widely known in Alberta as a rancher and big game hunter. He was an honorary colonel in the Canadian Black Watch Regiment.

Born in 1883 in McArthur, Ohio, during the 1930's he organized ventures in oil, mining and industry throughout the world.

He incorporated and was chairman of the board of Champlain Oil Company of Montreal, now a subsidiary of Imperial Oil. While he ran the company, Prime Minister Pierre Trudeau's father was one of his vice-presidents.

Between 1936 and 1939 he brought a radium mine into production at Great Bear Lake, and established the first North American radium refinery at Port Hope, Ontario, breaking the Belgian Congo's monopoly in the mineral.

The property provided uranium for Canadian and U.S. atomic energy programs during the Second World War.

The New Yorker magazine once called him the dean of this continent's big game hunters. He hunted on every continent and he is credited with having shot the world's record elephant in Kenya. He published two books about hunting.

In 1937 he sponsored an expedition to explore the Mackenzie District. A range of mountains on the Yukon-North West Territories border bears his name.

Colonel Snyder first visited Alberta in 1903, and while on a hunting expedition in the Peace River district in 1923 decided he wanted to retire here. He bought a ranch near Sundre in 1942. After it was destroyed by fire in 1955 he moved to Calgary, building a house on Anderson Road and 14 St. S.W.

He is survived by his wife Louise, who lives in Tucson Ariz.

BIBLIOGRAPHY

Addison, W.D. and Associates. Nahanni National Park Historical Resources Inventory. Interviews with Gus Kraus, Raymond M. Patterson, Albert Faille and Bill Clark.

Bailar, John Christian III. Correspondence with John Harris.

Berton, Pierre. The Mysterious North. Toronto: McClelland-Stewart, 1956

Bolyard, Dudley. Correspondence with John Harris.

Bolyard, Dudley. Preliminary Geologic Reconnaissance in the Logan Mountains, Northwest Territories. 1953. Unpublished Manuscript, supposedly in the Library of the Canadian Museum of Nature and the Library of the Department of Geology, Yale University, but now evidently lost.

Bolyard, Dudley. "The Yale Logan Expedition." Canadian Alpine Journal 36 (1953): 40 - 53.

Calgary Power Ltd. "Col. Harry Snyder — Big Game Hunter." Here's Alberta 23 (n.d.): 25-26.

Cody, William J. "A Tribute to Hugh Miller Raup, 1901 - 1995." The Canadian Field Naturalist 112 (1998): 557-564.

Col. H. M. Snyder Dies in Arizona." Calgary Herald 30 March 1972: 14.

Dalziel, George C. F. Book Manuscript in possession of his daughter, Sherry Bradford.

Finch, David. R.M. Patterson: A Life of Great Adventure. Calgary: Rocky Mountain Books, 2000.

Flook, Donald. Correspondence with John Harris.

Flook, Donald. "H. Snyder Expedition -- Upper South Nahanni River, August 1952."

Karl and David Raup on the Mackenzie River, 1939.

Flook, Donald. "Marten in the Central Mackenzie Region, Season 1952 - 53." WLT 2.77. 9 pages.

Goodwin, George G. "8000 Miles of Northern Wilderness." Natural History May 1936: 421-34.

Goodwin, George G. "Buffalo Hunt — 1935." Natural History Sept. 1935: 156-64.

Goodwin, George G. "The Snyder East Africa Expedition (videorecording)." American Museum of Natural History, 1939. <voyager@nimidi.amnh.org>

Goodwin, George G. "The Snyder Mountains." Natural History Dec. 1937: 750- 80.

LaGreca, Scott. Correspondence with John Harris.

Lambart, H. F. "The Harry Snyder Canadian Expedition, 1937." Canadian Alpine Journal XXV (1937): 1 - 18.

Laytha, Edgar. North again for Gold: Birth of Canada's Arctic Empire. New York: Frederick A. Stokes Co., 1939.

Martyn, Howell. Correspondence with John Harris.

O'Hara, Larry. "Three Youths Have Wild Trip through Wild Nahanni Valley." Edmonton Journal (15 August 1952): 2.

Raup, David. Correspondence with John Harris.

Raup, Hugh Miller. "Botanical Exploration of the Mackenzie Mountains." Arnold Arboretum Bulletin of Popular Information. Series 4, Vol. VII, No. 13 (15 Dec. 1939): 69-72.

Raup, Hugh Miller. Sargentia VI: The Botany of Southwestern Mackenzie. Arnold Arboretum, 1947.

RCMP Divisional File T517 - 5. [On the disappearance of Joe Mulholland and Bill Eppler]

Scotter, G. Correspondence with John Harris.

Shamp, Dick. Correspondence with John Harris.

Shaw, Const. T. E. G. "Valley of No Return." RCMP Quarterly 25.3 (3 Jan. 1960) n.p. Circulated by the Division of Tourism, Government of the NWT.

Simpson, Louise. Information Service, Earth Sciences Information Centre. Correspondence re. Howard Frederick Lambart. 14 Dec. 1999.

Snyder, Harry. "Exploring the Upper Nahanni River and Snyder Mountains in 1937." Canadian Geographical Journal 15 (1937): 169-202.

Snyder, Harry.   <u>Snyder's Book of Big-Game Hunting</u>.
Greenberg, 1950.

Soper, James H. Correspondence with John Harris.

Soper, James H. Diary: The Arnold Arboretum Expedition to
the Mackenzie Mountains. 1939.

W. W. F.   "In Memoriam: H.F.J. Lambart, 1880 - 1946."
<u>Canadian Alpine Journal</u> XXXIX. 2 (June, 1946): 284-85.